ORAL ROBERTS'
best sermons and stories

ORAL ROBERTS'

best sermons and stories

As presented in his
Great Evangelistic Campaigns
Around the World

1956
Oral Roberts
Tulsa, Oklahoma
U. S. A.

First Printing 50,000 Copies, April 1956

LIBRARY OF CONGRESS CATALOG CARD NO. 56-8451
PRINTED IN THE UNITED STATES OF AMERICA

Contents

ORAL ROBERTS'
best sermons and stories

Jesus of Nazareth

1

Jesus therefore, knowing all things that should come upon him, went forth, and said unto them, Whom seek ye? They answered him, Jesus of Nazareth. Jesus saith unto them, I am he (JOHN 18:4,5).

Jesus came at the lowest tide of human history, in the last fading, flickering light of the old law of Moses. He came at the least propitious hour of history when the eyes of the world were upon another man, Caesar, who ruled in Rome and kept men in bondage throughout the earth. The people of the world were not looking for Jesus of Nazareth. They were seeking a way of escape from the heavy hand of Caesar. It was not a time of miracles. Religion had lost its anointing. It seemed the very doors of Heaven had been closed.

At this time John the Baptist stepped out and cried, "He is coming!" Soon he was attracting the attention of multitudes of people, but John himself performed no miracle. He was the forerunner of Christ. Through a miracle he had been conceived in the old age of his parents, but he himself knew no miracle.

Jesus came with the crowd to the River Jordan, waded out into the water and said to John, "Baptize me." After John baptized him Jesus climbed up the bank, opened Heaven, let men hear God's voice, and went hurrying toward mankind as fast as he could to set them free. He returned to Galilee and in a few short weeks made the shore of the Sea of Galilee the front street of the world. Millions turned their attention away from Caesar and began looking to Jesus Christ of Nazareth. His miracles were the talk of the hour. The lame were walking, the blind were seeing, the dumb were speaking, the deaf were hearing, bread was being multiplied, water was being turned into wine, nature was being subdued, Heaven was being opened, angels were visiting men. He stirred the imagination of all mankind. How did he do it?

First, he burst forth from the crowd and opened Heaven to all men. Now, there are many who break away from the crowd, but few who break forth and open Heaven. That is the difference. Jesus of Nazareth not only broke forth from the crowd but he opened Heaven. The Bible says when he came up out of the water the heavens opened. He had been in Heaven. He had just come from Heaven. He knew what Heaven was. He knew it was the fulfillment of every man's wish. Yes, he knew Heaven. And he began to share his knowledge with the whole human race.

You know, there is something selfish about people. A little boy gets a bag of candy, and he wants to eat it all by himself. We get something, and we want it ourselves. We don't want anyone else to have it. But Jesus came from the greatest kingdom and said, "Here it is. I open Heaven to the human family." There are many men who close Heaven, but Jesus opened it to the family of man.

There is something marvelous about a door, especially if it is open to you. It is terrible if it is closed to you. My wife and I were driving through Atlanta, Georgia, when our first child was a baby. It was midnight. Atlanta is a large city; we got lost and couldn't find anybody to ask our way. So we just wound and wound through that town until three or four o'clock in the morning with no place to stay. The baby was crying. We were tired, and the door was closed. I'll remember that for a long time. It's an awful thing to see something good and have the door shut in your face; to drive through a town at night when you are ready to go to sleep and there is no hotel or motel open; to go into an area where you don't know a soul and you are out of money and the door is closed; or, in your poverty to come to the homes of the rich, but the door is locked. It's a wonderful thing to see the door open. Jesus opens the door.

In the Bible he says, "I place before you an open door." My friend, he opens the door and says, "Come in." That is Jesus of Nazareth.

Second, not only did Jesus of Nazareth break forth from the crowd and open Heaven to all men, but he immediately joined himself to the human family and began casting devils out of men.

Now Jesus recognized the devil's power in people, because it is the devil's power that makes people as they are—full of hate, sin, war, strife, sickness, and disease. He came against the devil's power and began casting devils out of people.

The Bible says, "We wrestle not against flesh and blood, but against principalities, against powers, against the rulers of the darkness of this world, against spiritual wickedness in high places" (Ephesians 6:12). Our fight is not with man. It is against the power of the devil in man. Jesus recognized the power of sin, demons, and evil spirits. He knew that people were mean and wicked and selfish and full of sickness and death because of the wicked devil loose in human society, and he came against the devil's power.

Jesus of Nazareth still recognizes the devil's power. Medical men and psychologists do not, as a whole, recognize the world of demons or the devil. But there are multiplied millions of evil spirits who are going to and fro seeking rest and finding none, except as they can enter a human being. Jesus came against these demons in men. He came against a legion of them in the man of Gadara. He healed the man and set him free. He set men and women free and the world heard them say, "I am myself again." Thousands of people could say, after meeting Jesus, "I am no longer bound by demons. My personality has been released. I am now a harmonious person. I am free inside and outside because Jesus of Nazareth has come into me."

I dreamed a dream a few nights ago. I saw a man who was demon possessed. The man was jerking and jumping and twisting and lunging and screaming at the top of his voice. I looked all about and saw that the people had run from him and were hiding on the fringes of an open arena. He was out in this open arena screaming and wanting to destroy. You could tell that he was tormented, that he didn't know what he was doing. He was possessed with something. He looked up and saw me. When he saw me, he screamed and came running toward me. For a moment fear swept through me. Then I got control of myself, and it seemed that I had been waiting for him for a long time, that I had been prepared for this moment. I rose up and the Spirit of God came into me like a flood. I reached out my hands toward him as he rushed up to me. Then I woke up. I knew God was showing me that my battle is not with man, but with the devil and demon spirits—cunning, evil, destroying spirits, who would destroy my ministry, who would destroy the gospel, and who would destroy the human race. I know that I am entering into a new phase of my ministry. For the first time this will be happening to me. I know I will have to meet this creature as he is multiplied millions of times in other people. I have had a preview of what we are to expect.

The third thing that Jesus of Nazareth did was to change the circumstances of man's failure and inability. When Jesus came to this earth he found that it was a world of impossibility. The power of God was not in action; the hand of man held sway. Caesar's might was feared by men. The power of God was conspicuous for its absence from the affairs of men. Because of the absence of God's power, men were not able to solve their problems. They came up against failure with no recourse. They came up against inability with no possibility of ever changing it. That is the world Jesus found. The ministry of John the Baptist did not make the lame walk or cause the blind to see. The ministry of John the Baptist was a local revival. It was a revival of repentance, of preparation. John's message said, "This is the beginning, but the big event is yet to come." That is all some of our churches have been doing, simply telling about the beginning of the big event. We are now ready for the big event!

Jesus of Nazareth came, and went forth on the Sea of Galilee while it was heaving and tossing like a drunken man; he walked on its waters, and made it a glassy road. He took the water from the waterpots and changed it into wine. He took the little boy's five loaves and two fishes, broke them, and fed five thousand men. He looked at impossibility, laughed in its face, and changed everything for the human family. He said to men, "When you stand up against failure and inability and futility, just believe God, and it shall be done."

Jesus changed everything. He changed everything for me. When I was 17 years old I lay flat on my back with tuberculosis. I stuttered and stammered so badly that nobody ever believed I would be a preacher. My own uncle said, "Why, he'll never preach. That poor little boy can't even talk." But Jesus of Nazareth changed things for me.

Jesus of Nazareth is a changer of men's circumstances. I don't believe that circumstances should stop God's people. I don't believe in *NO.* I don't like my men to come to me and say, "Brother Roberts, this can't be done." I don't like them to come to me and say, "This man won't do it." If he won't do it, God has another man who will. That's the way I believe it. I believe that circumstances are ours, that we don't belong to circumstances. I believe that failure and inability are foreign words to God's people. We are more than conquerors through him who loved us.

Fourth, in three short years he showed men a new way of life. He gave men a principle to live by. He said, "I am meek and lowly in heart." He did not give men a way of nonresistance, which was Mahatma Gandhi's way. Men were not to withdraw from life. Meekness is not nonresistance. Meekness is not being something for people to tread upon. Meekness is dynamic. Meekness is submission to God, so that God will break forth through you and do his mighty works.

Meekness and faith in God! Men in Jesus' time didn't know meekness and they didn't know faith. Rome was brutal and cruel. Religion didn't have any love. Religious leaders were ready to kill Christ at the very first opportunity. But Jesus gave us a way of life by which we can submit ourselves to God and he will plead our cause. We can have faith in God and he will change things for us. He has given us a new way of life.

Then he announced two things. First, *he was giving his*

power to those who believed in him. Second, *he would personally return to this earth.*

Now the world has come to accept the idea that this man lived. During his life, the world certainly didn't accept him. The world was forced to realize that there *was* a Jesus of Nazareth because he stirred the world. He captured the imagination of men. Even those who killed him never were able to suppress the truth of the resurrection. The Roman soldiers were heard to say, "Truly, this is the Son of God."

But after realizing that this man could do all these things, the world got the shock of its life when Jesus stepped out and said, "My disciples will do the same things that I have done, and greater things than these." Matthew the tax collector, Peter the fisherman, and those various ones would have his power. They, too, would break forth from the crowd and open Heaven to men. They would cast devils out of men. The disciples, too, would show that God is good, that God is not against any men or any race. They would heal the sick, change the circumstances of men, and do the mighty works of Jesus of Nazareth. Jesus of Nazareth reached forth his hands and gave the power of God to his disciples so they could reach forth their hands and give the power of God to humanity. It is a wonderful thing!

They killed Jesus, but the world soon discovered that he had risen up in a million different places; that when they took Jesus and nailed him to a cross, they could not destroy him, because he reappeared through his disciples' lives. Instead of killing one man, they multiplied him millions of times, because he transmitted his nature and power to his disciples. He is being multiplied again today as never before.

He said that he would return to this earth personally. This electrified his disciples and alerted the world. He told in exact detail of his second coming. He said it would be as quick as the lightning.

What does all this mean to us?

First, it means a resurgence of faith in the human heart in the last days. The alpha and omega must meet. The alpha is the beginning of the alphabet, and omega is the ending. He was in the alpha; we are in the omega. The beginning was glorious; the ending shall be supernatural. The resurgence of faith that Christ brought to mankind shall be multiplied thousands of times in these last days. The thing that people feel in their hearts today is Jesus of Nazareth. It is the world saying, "We seek Jesus of Nazareth." It is Christ saying, "I am he."

Second, there will be an acceleration of the works of Jesus. Jesus of Nazareth is to reappear in his disciples in the last days. Jesus is to be revealed in me and in you in such a way that when the world comes looking and saying, "Where is Jesus of Nazareth?" we can say, "Here he is. This is he!"

When they entered the Garden of Gethsemane, they were led by a man who knew where Jesus was and who he was. When they came near him, Jesus said, "Whom seek ye?"

They said, "Jesus of Nazareth."

Jesus said, "I am he."

(That time is coming again. Mankind is saying, "We seek Jesus of Nazareth.")

When they saw him and heard his words, they fell back like they were slapped down by an invisible hand. Their heads struck the ground. There is power in the name of Jesus of Nazareth—tremendous power!

The third thing it means to us today is the reliving and regiving of Jesus of Nazareth to all men, which means the mass miracle is about to happen. Jesus said, "Greater things shall ye do because I go to my Father," and these "greater things" are about to happen. The climax of the greater things is dawning, and it can mean only one thing—the mass miracle. It means healing on a mass scale. It will mean healing for thousands at one time. It will mean a crowd the size of my tent audiences healed in one moment. It will mean a whole church healed in one night.

My first meeting in Denver, Colorado, was in an auditorium. One evening before I left to preach, the Lord came to me in my room and spoke with me about the end of time and the coming of Christ. Here are some of his words. He said, "Son, there remains a healing for the sick body of my bride. I have raised you up for this purpose, to help bring healing to the body of my bride." Then the Lord gave me a picture of a boy and a girl about to get married, when suddenly the girl became unmarriageable. You know, we have health laws whereby a couple has to be examined. If they have certain diseases, the marriage is prohibited. Jesus showed me that there was a condition which made his bride at this point unmarriageable, and it must be healed.

You can imagine how that was misunderstood seven years ago, so I quit telling it. But now I think we are far enough along in the Lord, all of us, that we will understand it. He said, "The body of my bride is sick," and he gave me a picture of the many ministers of the gospel who carry in their bodies serious afflictions which hinder them very much. He showed me that the people who are saved are just as sick as the people who are not saved, and he said, "There remains a healing." He didn't say how much. He didn't tell me it would be a perfect healing. I can only repeat what I was told. He said, "There remains a healing for the sick body of my bride," and he gave me a picture of a healthy, happy, joyous girl who was fully marriageable. He said that was the bride he was going to marry.

I don't say for one moment that your being sick would keep you from going to Heaven or being in the bride if you are saved. That is not mine to judge. But I will say this:

Any real Christian who loves God, who wants to work for God, and wants to be in the bride of Christ would like to be well and strong, and be able to do God's service and bring children into the kingdom of God.

Now I see this demon-possessed man whom I saw in my dream. I see him in the dream as he is in the open arena, as the people have fled from him and are scared. I see him as he jumps, lurches, and cries, and opens and closes his hands trying to get hold of somebody to rend and destroy. I can see myself again as the spirit of fear swept through me and I was shocked by it. Then the Spirit of God rose in me, and I stood up to go fight with him.

The hour has come. The battle will be joined, and I prophesy that from this hour until the coming of the Lord this dream will represent the people of God who are going out into the arena to fight with this power, to deliver the people. Jesus of Nazareth will reappear, not only in his rapture and revelation but he will be revealed in us. The world will see Jesus of Nazareth again!

How You Can Know You Are Saved

2

We know that we have passed from death unto life, because we love the brethren (1 JOHN 3:14).

Many people would like to know beyond a shadow of a doubt that they are saved by Jesus Christ. I've never known or seen such interest as people are showing today in knowing that they are saved. Person after person writes to me, saying, "Brother Roberts, please tell me how I may know that I am really saved."

Recently there was a young woman who came before me for prayer. She said, "Brother Roberts, I have been in pain for a very long time. But I can stand the pain if you will show me how I can know I am saved." I prayed for her, and the Lord not only took the pain away, but she said, "Now I know that I am saved."

There was a man in one of my meetings who said,

"Brother Roberts, I'm sick but I came here for something else also. I am a member of a church, and active in that church, but I have never been saved. I want to know tonight that I am saved by Jesus Christ." Thank God, he was saved.

I would rather know that I am saved, that God is my Saviour and I am his child, than to know anything else in the whole wide world. For Jesus says, "What shall it profit a man, if he shall gain the whole world, and lose his own soul?" (Mark 8:36).

You say, "Brother Roberts, what do you mean by being saved?" Well, that's the term we use to express Jesus Christ's coming into our heart, or being converted from sin, or being born again by the Spirit of God. I mean that God comes into your heart, that he forgives your sins, that you surrender yourself to him, and you know that Jesus is your personal Saviour—that's what I mean when I say "*getting saved and knowing that you are saved.*"

How can you know? There is a way to know. I want to say that very definitely—*you can know that you are saved;* not from what I say or what someone else says, but from the Word of God. The Bible is the only authority in Heaven and earth that really shows us the way to be saved.

First, you may know that you are saved if your repentance has been caused by godly sorrow. The Bible says that godly sorrow worketh repentance to salvation. There are a lot of people who are sorry for what they have done and they repent, but they don't repent because of godly sorrow. They repent because they've been caught, or because suddenly they are confronted with their wrong and they're terribly embarrassed about it. But the prodigal son who went away from home and found himself at the end of the way said, "I will arise and go to my father, and will say unto him, Father, I have sinned against heaven, and before thee, and am no more worthy to be called thy son: make me as one of thy hired servants" (Luke 15:18,19). Now this is the kind of repentance that is caused by godly sorrow. You're sorry you have sinned; you are sorry because you've done wrong; not because you're caught or embarrassed, but you're sorry because you sinned against God. You've sinned against Heaven; you've sinned against your fellow man; you've sinned against yourself and now you know you've done the wrong thing.

When you repent like this you actually make a change. The prodigal not only said, "I have sinned against Heaven," but also, "I'll arise and go back to my father. I'll no longer be a prodigal." Your purpose is changed. You stop the downward course of your life. You return to God. You live a new life. That kind of repentance is brought by godly sorrow.

Judas Iscariot repented. But do you know when he repented? When he realized that he had sold his Lord for thirty pieces of silver and in that sale he was responsible for his early death. He was not sorry that he had been greedy. It's true he took the money back. He repented over the crime, but he made no change. He didn't go to the Lord Jesus and say, "I've sinned against Heaven. I've sinned against thee." He simply took a rope and tied it around his neck and committed suicide. This is the kind of sorrow or repentance that does no good. In fact, it really does evil. Many people who repent in the wrong way wind up taking their own lives or getting into further trouble. You must repent because you have sinned against God and against Heaven, and because you know you've done the wrong thing. You may know that you're saved when you realize that you have repented because of godly sorrow.

The second way you can know you are saved is when you have believed on a Person—Jesus Christ of Nazareth.

Getting saved is not believing some creed. Getting saved is not accepting a certain philosophy of life. Getting saved is not joining a church. Getting saved is not being baptized in water. Getting saved is believing on a Person, Jesus Christ of Nazareth.

When you get saved it is true that you *will* accept the Lord's creed, you *will* receive a new philosophy of life, you *will* be baptized in water, you *will* associate yourself with some good church. But those things do not save you. You are saved by the Man, Jesus Christ of Nazareth. Jesus of Nazareth is the Saviour. The church is not the Saviour; water baptism is not the Saviour; a philosophy of life is not the Saviour; a different creed is not the Saviour; reformation is not the Saviour. Jesus is the Saviour. It is said that the schools inform, the reformatories reform, but only Christ can transform. The Bible says there is no other name under Heaven given among men whereby we must be saved except the name of Jesus of Nazareth. You're saved by a Person.

Once there was a boy who fell out with his father who was equally filled with hate for him. The boy, angry and offended, stalked out of the house and said, "I'll never come back." The weeks passed during which the mother hoped that her son would get over it and hurry back home. The weeks stretched into months and the months into years, and the boy did not return. She said to her husband, "Now this is not right. I want you to write a letter and tell our son to come home." He said, "I'll not do it!" So she worried and fretted like mothers will do, and in that weakened condition she took an incurable disease. The doctor said to her husband, "Your wife is going to die." When she discovered how sick she was she said to her husband, "Please do not deny me the privilege of seeing my son one more time." Still unrelenting himself, he wrote the letter. The boy returned as quickly as he could, rushed in the house and didn't even speak to his father or look at him. Instead he went into the bedroom, fell down upon his mother's body and sobbed and cried, "Mother, don't die, don't die!" She pushed him off her body and looked up over the other side of the bed and there was her husband. She saw they wouldn't look at each other, or wouldn't speak to each other. She knew she didn't have much time left and she took hold of their hands and with her last bit of strength she pulled her husband and her son together across her dying body. She breathed a feeble sigh and was gone. The father looked at the son and the son at the father; and broken by mutual sorrow, they were reconciled across the body of the one whom they both loved.

In like manner Jesus Christ of Nazareth, Son of God and Son of man, upon the cross, reached up with the right hand of his divine nature and took hold of the hand of an offended God. With the left hand of his pure and bleeding humanity he reached down and took hold of the hand of offending sinners. With the last bit of strength he had he pulled man up and God down, reconciling man to God and God to man. Since that time the cross has been the perfect meeting place between God and man. Jesus of Nazareth is the One who can save you. He is the only One who can save you because he is the One who reconciled your soul unto its Creator. Therefore, you must be saved by a Person. You must be saved by the Son of God. You're not saved by man. You're saved by a Man. God gave the brightest Jewel. He gave the Pearl of great price. He gave the glittering Diamond. He gave his only begotten Son, and he said that "God so loved the world, that he gave his only begotten Son, that whosoever believeth in him should not perish, but have everlasting life" (John 3:16). God didn't give a creed or philosophy–he gave his Son. He gave a Man. You must believe in Jesus Christ. When you have believed on him, you can know that you're saved.

The first thing that you do to know that you're saved is to repent of your sins because of godly sorrow. The second thing you do is to believe in a Person, Jesus Christ of Nazareth; and third, receive the Lord Jesus. The Bible says in John 1:12, "As many as received him, to them gave he power to become the sons of God." Now you may repent of your sins, you may believe in Jesus Christ, but until you receive him, until Christ actually enters your soul, you are not saved, because the point of power is reached when you receive Christ. "As many as received him, to them gave he power." When you receive the Son of God into your thinking and believing, into your heart and life, then the power of God goes into action. The most powerful experience known to man is when you receive Christ, for the power of God is unleashed in your life–the power of God that breaks the cord that separates you from God, the power of God that breaks the devil's hold on your life, the power of God that saves you from sin, the power of God that lifts you from the death of sins and trespasses, the power of God that translates you from the kingdom of night to the kingdom of light, the power of God that snatches you from the devil's hand and puts you in the hands of God, the power of God that banishes your dark night and puts the sun to shining in your soul, the power of God that separates you from wrong company and makes angels your guardians and saints your brothers and sisters, and Heaven your home, and God your Father, and Jesus Christ your Saviour. When you receive Christ, power is given unto you. It puts a spring in your step, a light in your eye, a shine on your face, a shout in your soul. It gives you something real. It separates you from this wicked world. It fills you with peace and joy and love. *You can know it when you receive Christ!*

Now I come to the fourth way that you may know you are saved. Confess Jesus Christ before men. The Bible says, "If thou shalt confess with thy mouth the Lord Jesus, and believe in thine heart that God hath raised him from the dead, thou shalt be saved." A young girl got saved in our tent campaign one night on the East Coast, and she was radiantly happy. Her face shone like an angel's. She was about the happiest girl I ever saw. She had come to the meeting in the company of her boy friend, and her first thought was to testify to this boy and confess her Saviour to him. She hurried down the aisle, went to her chair and sat down, put her hand over on his arm and said, "Jim, I got saved. I never knew before what it was to be saved. Jesus is in my heart. I've never been so happy in my life. Jim, I want you to go to the prayer tent right now and let Jesus come into your heart." He laughed in her face. She said, "You don't understand. You just don't understand how wonderful it is," and he laughed again. She didn't know what to do. He began to mock her. She said, "Jim, are you serious? Don't you respect God?" He mocked her again. "All right," she said and stood up. She looked back down and said, "Jim, if you won't go to Heaven with me, I'm not going to hell with you," and she walked away.

When Jesus comes into your heart, you will stand up for him, you will testify for him, you will witness for him. Not everybody loses a friend but some do. I lost some friends, but for every friend I lost God gave me thousands of friends in their place. Since I've been saved the best people in the world have become my friends. Many of them appreciate my stand for Christ. Some of them don't but I love them all anyway. I have made up my mind that I'm going to be a Christian. I'm going to serve God.

Now, if thou shalt confess with thy mouth the Lord Jesus —if you are ashamed to confess Christ, how can you know you are saved? Some say, "I don't know it." Well perhaps you are not confessing him with your mouth. Had you thought about that? If you don't know you're saved, what's the good of having a bank account? What is the world worth to you if you lose your soul? Where are you going to spend eternity if you don't know that you're saved? Do you know that Jesus said, "If you're ashamed to confess me before men, I'll be ashamed to confess you before my Father and the holy angels in Heaven"?

You can know that you're saved if you are proud to confess him before men, if with joy you stand up and say, "Yes, Jesus is my Saviour. Jesus is in my heart."

Confessing him with your mouth is important. It's just as important as believing on him with your heart, for both of them are necessary because God has saved you and come into your heart. Can you honestly say, "I'm confessing him with my mouth, I'm standing up for the Lord"?

We know we're saved when we have repented because of godly sorrow. Second, we know we're saved when we have believed on a Person, Jesus Christ of Nazareth. Third, we know that we are saved when we have received that Person, Jesus of Nazareth, into our hearts, for then we receive the power to become a child of God. And fourth, we know that we are saved when we witness to him, when we confess the Lord with our mouths. But the most important thing is that you have become a new creature. The Bible says, "If any man be in Christ, he is a new creature: old things are passed away; behold, all things are become new" (2 Cor. 5:17). You're not your old self any more, you're brand-new. You're new to yourself, you're new to your fellow man, you're new to your family. Old things have passed away.

You have passed from death unto life because you love the brethren. You love the people of God. There are some people who are not saved. They may say they are saved, but we know they are not saved because they don't love Christian people. They don't like the touch of Jesus Christ. They don't like Heaven. They don't talk like they're saved. When you know you are saved you don't enjoy the company of people who are not saved. You're not at home with people who are smoking and drinking and cursing and lying and cheating and living like the devil. You like to live around people whose heart is clean, whose conversation is clean. You like that old-fashioned Holy Ghost feeling. You like to hear people testify for the Lord. You like an anointed sermon from the servant of God. You like to see people healed and saved. You like to gather with people and sing and pray and shout and have a wonderful time and *know* you've passed from death unto life, because you love the brethren.

Also, "Therefore being justified by faith, we have peace with God" (Rom. 5:1). You become a new creature not only because you've passed from death unto life and you love the brethren, but because you have peace with God. The old struggle that has been in your heart has been taken out. That tenseness because of unforgiven sins has been removed and you feel so relieved. You're released. Something has entered you from above. Jesus abides in your heart and you know that you are saved.

God Has an Appointment with You

3

Now Moses kept the flock of Jethro his father in law, the priest of Midian: and he led the flock to the backside of the desert, and came to the mountain of God, even to Horeb. And the angel of the Lord appeared unto him in a flame of fire out of the midst of a bush: and he looked, and, behold, the bush burned with fire, and the bush was not consumed. And Moses said, I will now turn aside, and see this great sight, why the bush is not burnt. And when the Lord saw that he turned aside to see, God called unto him out of the midst of the bush, and said, Moses, Moses. And he said, Here am I. And he said, Draw not nigh hither: put off thy shoes from off thy feet, for the place whereon thou standest is holy ground. Moreover he said, I am the God of thy father, the God of Abraham, the God of Isaac, and the God of Jacob. And Moses hid his face; for he was afraid to look upon God. And the Lord said, I have surely seen the affliction of my people which are in Egypt, and have heard their cry by reason of their task-masters; for I know their sorrows. . . . Come now there-

fore, and I will send thee unto Pharaoh, that thou mayest bring forth my people the children of Israel out of Egypt (EXODUS 3:1–7,10).

The time had come for God to deliver the children of Israel out of Egyptian bondage. He chose a man, a human instrument, by the name of Moses. Moses misunderstood the purpose of God. He rose up in his own strength and went forth to set the people free. He did not go with God's anointing or God's supernatural power. He did not have a miraculous visitation from God to inspire him. Moses went without a changed life, and he made the biggest failure of his life. In fact, he killed a man and had to flee the country. He marred the blueprint of God to set his people free at that time. He ran away as fast as he could to the backside of the desert.

In 1954, I flew to the Holy Land. One of the trips which I took was from Cairo to Jerusalem in an airplane. I flew over a major portion of the barren waste that is called the desert of that part of the country. Looking down from the air, I saw the most desolate, the most barren, part of the earth my eyes have ever looked upon. That is where Moses wound up. Wandering out there in the desert, he became a total failure, a fugitive from God, a runaway from the Lord.

But Moses had an appointment with God, and God had an appointment with Moses. Moses found this appointment in the desert. God had tried to keep his appointment with him in the palace, in his home, in the land of Egypt. But somehow Moses had not understood. Now, Moses, a total failure, found that God still had an appointment with him. Why did God come to him in the desert? Why did God come to him at this particular time? It was the only time God could come. Moses, for the first time in his life, was willing to listen to God. He was willing to entertain an appointment with God. Before, he thought that he had the ability, the spirit, and the power to deliver the children of Israel. He didn't feel he needed a miraculous visitation. Now he was at the end of his own strength, at the backside of the desert, and a total failure. There God was able to find him, to talk with him, and to keep his appointment with him.

Why are there so many human failures today? Men and women have not kept their appointments with God. Men and women have thought that they could run their lives without God, that they didn't need God's anointing, or a miraculous visitation of the Lord. They felt that they had the answer to their own problems. They could rise and conquer; they were the masters of their own destiny. They would not keep their appointment with God. Therefore, God was not able to keep his appointment with them, and they became failures. You may not be in the backside of a literal desert, but you are at the end of your own strength. If you have not kept your appointment with God, if you have not talked with God and he with you, if you have not met God, if God has not come to you, then you are a failure. You may have a million dollars, you may have a beautiful home, you may have contacts with this one and that one, you may have a fine wife and children, you may have an excellent job and career, but if you haven't kept your appointment with God, you are a failure!

Moses had an appointment with God. In the backside of the desert and a total failure, Moses was in the mood and the attitude to keep that appointment. Why don't we listen to God when everything is going well? When everything is high, wide, and handsome, man throws out his chest, squares his shoulders and says, "I don't need any help from anybody. I don't need the help of God. Why should I pray?" But you know, the curtain always falls. The sun goes down and the shadows creep in. This happens to every person who will not keep his appointment with God.

Moses was in the backside of the desert when God appeared. God kept his appointment with Moses by appearing to him through a burning bush. Moses was keeping the flock of his father-in-law Jethro. One day in the backside of the desert, his eye was attracted by a burning bush. It was not an uncommon scene at that time because on the hot, burning, shimmering sands of the desert any bush might suddenly be aflame with fire. But this was an uncommon sight because the bush kept burning and it wasn't consumed. Moses said, "This is unusual. I've seen many bushes on fire, but they all burned up. I wonder why this bush isn't burning up? I think I'll turn aside and see this great sight." All of a sudden, the voice of God spoke to him from the burning bush and said, "Moses, take off your shoes. You are standing on holy ground."

This bush is one of the most miraculous things in the Bible. The bush itself is not a miracle, but God in the bush is a miracle. You may not be a miracle, I may not be a miracle, but when God comes into us we become a living miracle. This bush was just a common little desert bush until the Lord came into it. The Lord made it flame and burn and shake and crackle. God made the bush shine and burn there in the desert. He made the bush contain his presence. In fact, God changed the nature of the bush.

It's not the nature of a bush to accommodate fire because fire is the stronger of the two. But God changed the nature of this bush so that it could contain him. God came into the bush and its leafy arms held God. From its boughs the voice of God spoke, and from its very heart came the message and plan of God. God said, "Moses, take off your shoes; you're standing on holy ground. Moses, I have heard the cry of my people. I have seen their sorrows and afflictions.

I shall send thee to Egypt to lead my people out of bondage." Moses could not see God, but he could hear God. He could feel God. All he could see was a burning bush, a bush that was flaming with the everlasting presence of the Lord God of Heaven and earth. It was the flame in the bush that showed him it was God. It was the flame in the bush that arrested his attention. The flame of God's presence still arrests the attention of mankind. The burning fire is the thing that stirs the imagination of mankind. That bush had its nature changed so that it could literally accommodate God. It contained God. The voice of God spoke from the bush, and the flame attracted the attention of this runaway, this total failure.

When God keeps his appointment with you he's going to do it by a miracle. God does not work in ordinary ways when he comes to you. God works in ordinary ways through nature, through people, through circumstances on this earth. But when he personally comes to you, he comes in no ordinary way. God comes in an extraordinary manner. You need not expect to receive salvation by turning over a new leaf. You need not expect to change your life by joining a church. You will change your life when God comes to you, when the flame burns in your heart, when you are arrested by the flaming presence of Jesus Christ of Nazareth. When God comes, he speaks. When God comes, he shines. His presence goes out from him into the people. He stirs the people and attracts them. When God comes, people *feel* him.

One woman said, "Brother Roberts, you don't mean to say I have to feel God to know I am saved?"

I said, "You most certainly do have to feel God to know you are saved."

Do you know how little you are? The Bible compares you to a grain of sand on the everlasting seashore, and God is so big that he holds the whole universe in the palm of his hand. If God is so big and you're so little, how could God come into you and you not know it? When God is so big and you're so little and the twain meet, something takes place. When God comes in and speaks the sin away and heals the disease and enters your being, *something* happens and you feel it. You know that the Lord has come.

This bush intrigues me. It was just a common bush. It didn't live on the front street. It wasn't in somebody's hothouse. It was not a special plant. It had no rare pedigree that could be traced back into centuries past. Until God came into it, it was just a little, unnoticed bush growing out on the backside of the desert. My friend, you don't have to be somebody special. You don't have to be "somebody come." You don't have to be somebody whose pedigree can be traced back several generations. You don't have to have a lot of money. You don't have to have an education. You don't have to have anything except the Lord, because when the Lord comes in he will glorify you. He glorified that little bush. It has been memorialized a thousand times and the perpetuity of it is insured for eternity. When God comes into you, common as you are, common and little and insignificant as I am, God gives us a perpetuity. God gives us an eternity. God comes into us and lifts our heads, raises our hands, and shines through us. He blazes the flames through us and speaks through us. He arouses the attention of the world through us, and blesses the people through us.

Until the Lord came into it, it was just a bush. But it was able to contain God. And if a bush could contain God, surely you, an eternal soul, can contain him. God, in his appointment with Moses, made Moses that burning bush. He set the bush on fire because he wanted Moses to be set on fire. He spoke through the bush as he wanted to speak through Moses. He came to that little, insignificant, no-account bush and set it on fire, because he wanted to come to the worst failure known in history, set him on fire, and send him back to deliver two million children of Israel out of the bondage of Egypt. God made Moses a burning bush. He changed his nature. The nature of Moses was a warring, struggling nature. He rose up in his own strength, discounting God's power, and said, "With these fists I'll deliver my people." He succeeded in killing one Egyptian and then had to run for his life.

A lot of people feel that they can live by their wits, that they can take their fists and knock somebody's block off. But you can't live like that. You've got to have God in you to live. God changed Moses' nature.

The next thing he did was to enter him by a miraculous visitation. God came into Moses so that when Moses spoke, it was God speaking. God put a rod in his hand as a point of contact and said, "Moses, stretch out your rod. When you stretch it out I'll stretch out my arm." And Moses went back as a burning bush.

All of a sudden Egypt was aroused by a burning bush. They looked out and saw an insignificant man who had run away, who had been a total failure, who had thrown his life away. But it was not the old Moses. It was a brand-new Moses who was on fire. It was a Moses who was flaming for the glory of God. Pharaoh looked up and saw him; the whole cabinet of Egypt saw him; the magicians of Egypt saw him; and the children of Israel saw him. They looked out and saw a bush burning in the desert. This time it was a man. That man contained God. God had come into him. When Moses spoke, it was God speaking. When Moses stretched forth his hand, it was God's hand outstretched. Moses performed mighty miracles. He shook that country. He led his people out with a high hand. Not even a dog barked when they left on that starless night. When they came to the Red Sea, he raised up his rod. The waters parted and they walked across dry-shod. He brought manna from Heaven and water from the flinty rock. This man became a burning bush. He stirred Egypt and delivered the people of God.

A little boy met me one night as I came into the tent, and there were tears streaming down his cheeks. He reached and got my hand and said, "Brother Roberts, give me your autograph." I wrote my name on a little piece of paper. He said, "Brother Roberts, do you think that I could ever be like you? Do you think I could preach like you? Do you think I could heal the people like that? Do you think a thousand would come up in one night and get saved when I preached?"

Well, how could I answer him? What could I say to a little ten-year-old boy? All I could think was if God could raise me up from a sick bed, if God could come to me when I was only a common bush and set me on fire, he could do it for anybody. I believe that. I don't believe there are any *special* folks. I don't believe that there are any special "I's." God wants an appointment with everybody. God has a mission for every human being. Everybody has a personal appointment with his Maker, who will reveal his will to them and let them know what he has in store for their life. I want you to understand that no matter how low we get in the humdrum of life, how mediocre we are, how insignificant our lives become, how low down on the ladder we slip or how deep into the pit we fall, the God of Heaven can set the bush on fire. The God of Heaven can come into us. The God of Heaven can pick us up. He can heal that stuttering tongue, that blind eye, that deaf ear, the crippled limb. God can heal that mind of yours. God can make you a flaming bush in the twentieth century. God has an appointment with everybody.

Moses had an appointment with God. God kept that appointment even though he had to go to the backside of the desert when Moses had reached his end. Friends, that's the best time you can have an appointment with God: when you are willing to have it, when you've reached the end of yourself, when you know that you must have the help of our wonderful God.

God appeared for his appointment with Moses in a burning bush, and in that bush he showed his miraculous power. He flamed and spoke and glorified his name. He gave Moses a blueprint of deliverance. He set his people free.

You know, God kept his appointment with me and I kept mine with him in 1947. When I think about how near I came to dying and what God is doing through my ministry today, it sends a ripple of excitement through my being. In 1947, God's appointment with me was in dreams. He showed me the human family. I saw something that most people have never seen. I saw the human family as God sees it. He said, "Son, I'm going to show you the human family as I see them." He showed me lost and suffering humanity. The thing that startled me was that the vast majority of people are lost and sick. I didn't know that. I thought that there was *some* sickness, but I found that the *majority* of all human beings are sick in some way. I found that everybody is sick except the person who has just been healed. I didn't know that before. Nearly everyone has some disease, some affliction, some form of sickness or illness in their body, mind, or soul. God let me hear the cry of humanity. God let me see the festering sores, the unresolved frustrations, the tormenting fears. Every night after my dream I'd wake up walking in my sleep, something which I'd never done before nor have done since. When I awoke I would find myself shaking, sobbing, and crying. My wife Evelyn found me like that about 4 o'clock one morning in the corner of the bathroom on my face sobbing and crying. I was asleep dreaming this dream, seeing and hearing these people. She tapped me on the shoulder and woke me up and asked me what I was doing. For the first time I told her my dream. We sat there on the side of the bed the rest of the night planning how I could really meet God, how I could keep my appointment with him, and how I could burn like this bush, how I could stir my generation, how I could take God's healing to my fellow man.

Every one of us has an appointment with God. He may come to you through a dream or a sermon. He may come to you through some still, small voice in the night. He may come to you as you walk alone in the woods down by the stream, as you wash dishes, or as you work at your job. He may come to you in a manner that I would not understand. The main thing is that you understand it. But God is going to come to you. You have an appointment with God.

The soul-saving campaigns that God gives us in the great tent cathedral is God's appointment with multitudes. Angels walk the grounds, the Lord walks the aisles, people feel the Holy Ghost and fire under the tent. Many people have said, "Brother Roberts, when I walk on the grounds I feel the presence of God." Nearly every stutterer that has come to our campaign to get healed received healing before ever getting to me. Many of them find they can talk without even being prayed for, for the atmosphere in the tent is charged with God's healing power. It is holy ground. How many people have felt a holiness, a reverence, and the presence of God as they entered the grounds or the big tent. People get healed out in the audience; people who have given up all hope of ever getting well get saved and healed in the tent. People go to my campaigns who have been members of churches for years but never knew before that they were saved.

This is your appointment. This is your moment to get saved and know it. This is your hour to be healed from the crown of your head to the soles of your feet. This is your hour to meet God and for God to meet you. This is your hour to be changed. This is your hour for a miraculous visitation from the Lord. This is your appointment with God.

4 You and I Together with God Can Change the World

The Spirit of the Lord is upon me, because he hath anointed me to preach the gospel to the poor; he hath sent me to heal the brokenhearted, to preach deliverance to the captives, and recovering of sight to the blind, to set at liberty them that are bruised, to preach the acceptable year of the Lord (LUKE 4:18,19).

Jesus of Nazareth came to this earth at the lowest tide in history. He came in the fading, flickering light of the old law of Moses. He stepped into a river of water, was baptized by man, climbed the bank and started toward the human race as fast as he could.

The world was not prepared for him. They were not expecting him to come. Rome held death's sway in the earth. There were no miracles taking place. Religion had been shorn of its power. It had lost its anointing. Throughout the earth there was a faithlessness in the hearts of the masses.

There were people who were praying, fasting, and believing. But the world was not praying. The world was not believing. The world was trying to survive from the cruelty of the Roman Empire.

John the Baptist, who presented Jesus Christ, had no miracles of his own. He did not present Christ as a miracle-worker. John the Baptist was a theologian. He was a man who had been raised up in the Jewish religion, and that is what he knew. But he was the ordained forerunner of Jesus Christ. God raised him up to announce his entrance upon the stage of human action.

But not even John realized the full significance of the coming of Jesus Christ. He presented Jesus in two ways: first, as the baptizer with the Holy Ghost, and then as the Lamb of God. The knowledge that John had was from God himself, but it was tempered by his religious knowledge. To John, Christ was two things. He was the baptizer with the Holy Ghost and fire and he was the Lamb which was to suffer. But Christ was so much more than those things. He was also the Lion of the tribe of Judah. He was the Baptizer, but he was also the Resurrection and the Life. John didn't see all these things because he was looking at him through his religious training. The greatest thing we have to fight today in our approach to God is our religious training—what somebody has told us about the Lord.

Jesus climbed up a river bank and walked to Galilee, and as he walked those rocky shores, he turned them into the front streets of the world. Within a matter of days he had released energy, ideals, and power into human society. Within a matter of weeks, he had crashed the headlines of the world. Within a matter of months, the human race was dizzy with the movement and excitement of this man. He captured the imagination of all mankind. He was to be a lamb, but he didn't capture their imagination as a lamb. He was to baptize with the Holy Ghost, but that day was to come after he had returned to his Father. How then did he stir man's imagination? How then did he make the sunny banks of Galilee the main streets of the whole world?

The first thing he did was be baptized in water. The spoken voice of Almighty God placed approval on his Son: "This is my beloved Son in whom I am well pleased." The next thing he did was go into a church where there was a man with an unclean spirit. The spirit screamed out, and Jesus called the demon out of the man and set him free and restored his mind. The fame of Jesus began to spread. He subdued the rolling waves and walked the waters of the Sea of Galilee. Then he took a little boy's lunch and blessed and broke it, and gave it to five thousand men and satisfied fully their appetite. He put his hands upon blind eyes and they came open, upon deaf ears and they were unstopped, upon crippled limbs and they were straightened. This man's power was felt like a liquid fire in the bodies, minds, and souls of men. He was not announced as a miracle-worker, for the man who introduced him did not know all that Christ was going to be and do in this world. But he had the way, the power, and the anointing, and within a short time the world was talking about Jesus Christ of Nazareth.

Then to further astound the world he called his disciples to him. He had gathered them from the far corners of the land. Some were fishermen, some were businessmen, some were farmers. He called these men to his side and in the presence of the world said, "I give you men my power. You're going to do these things—you will heal the sick, cast out devils, raise the dead, cleanse the leper. You will do all these mighty things." And they did it! In the presence of the world these men went out in the name of Jesus, laid their hands upon the sick and afflicted and set them free and made them whole by faith in God.

Before he left this world, he further startled humanity by calling his disciples and saying to them, "Greater things than these shall ye do. When I go back to my Father I will give you the Holy Ghost and through him you will do even greater things." Jesus released energy into man's life that man never knew existed. He released ideas that caught the fancy of humanity and finally caused them to sit up and take notice. He released his power so that power flowed out of him like a river into people's bodies and they were healed of blindness, deafness, leprosy, deformity—whatever diseases they had. He even sent one of his disciples fishing and the fish had money in its mouth to pay his taxes. He startled the world in every way. Jesus changed the world in three years. He spent thirty years in preparation, worked only three, and turned the world upside down.

He released ideas into the world which caused others to begin to study him. People who had never made an impact upon anybody, people who had known no miracle of their own, who had lived little drab lives and didn't amount to a hill of beans, looked at this man, listened to him, and they began to change the world.

One of them was the Syrophenician woman. She was a Gentile, and in those days the Jewish people looked down upon the Gentile people as a race of dogs. But a little child was demon possessed, mentally ill. The mother heard of Jesus and immediately crossed the borders of her country, came into Palestine on the front streets of the world and found Jesus. If you wanted to walk the front streets of the world in those days, you had to go where Jesus was. She found him, rushed up and declared to him what her need was, and the Bible said he answered her not a word. Finally he said, "Woman, it is not right to give the children's bread to dogs."

Immediately there flashed through her mind what he

meant. She said, "Truth, Lord. That's right. The master doesn't give the bread of the children to his dog; but he does give a crumb. Give me a crumb, Lord."

He said, "O woman, great is thy faith: go thy way, it shall be done unto thee even as thou wilt." And her child was healed that very hour.

This woman unlocked something for the human family. She changed the world. Until that time healing was considered a luxury, something the average person could not have. A lot of people still feel that way.

But this woman discovered two things. First, *healing is the children's bread.* Bread is the staff of life and man cannot live without bread. Yet man shall live by bread. Not by bread alone, but he shall live by bread. *Healing* here is *bread;* it is *the children's bread.* We have to have bread every day. So the Syrophenician opened up a new world for us all, that there is *daily healing in this world.*

Second, *it's for everybody who will become a follower of God.* She changed the world! She changed it for me. She changed it for you. There were people who told me to my face, "Oral, it may not be God's will to heal you."

So I can step out in my generation and offer hope to every man, woman, and child—black, white, red, yellow, and brown—all nations, rich and poor, high and low, ignorant and smart. I can offer the healing of God to every person who is in this world, knowing that God is willing to heal every one of them. That makes a bigger man out of me! I can connect myself with a God, who is so good that he is willing to heal anybody, no matter who he is. It makes me feel good even to know this God and to walk and talk with him on earth.

Look at the centurion in the eighth chapter of Matthew's Gospel. He came running up to Christ and knelt at his feet. He was a Roman army captain, and he had never before knelt at any man's feet, except Caesar's. But this time he sees one greater than Caesar. It is force bowing to meekness, armed might before the unarmed, the proud uniform of war before the seamless robe, the sword before the healing hand.

He said, "Lord, my servant lieth at home, sick of the palsy, grievously tormented."

Christ said, "I will come and heal him."

He said, "Oh, no, Lord, you don't have to *come* to heal him. I am also a man in authority, and I know what authority is. I say to this soldier, 'You go,' and he goes; to another, 'Come,' and he comes. Lord, you have authority above all authority. You have power above all power. You don't have to go; you don't have to come; you speak the word. There's no distance in prayer, Jesus. You just stand up here and speak, and my servant will be healed over yonder miles away."

That centurion changed the world for millions. Up to that time, people thought that they had to be in the physical presence of Jesus to get healed. Since Christ's ministry on this earth was only a little over three years, and as he could be in only one place at a time, you can imagine how few people, comparatively speaking, could be healed by Christ. Also, when he moved his physical presence from earth to Heaven, that left you and me out altogether.

But this man proved to the world that there is no distance in prayer. Christ said, "I have not seen so great faith, no not in Israel. Go thy way. As thou hast believed so be it done unto thee." And his servant was healed in the selfsame hour.

There is no distance in prayer! I didn't know that. I knew it, and yet I didn't know it. I come home between meetings to rest. By rest, I mean I do a different kind of work. I come home to do the work which must be done there. I record the broadcasts, go to the studio and preach and pray. Do you know a man can go into a studio and preach a sermon and pray a prayer of faith and put it on the air in Europe or Africa, and people will be healed by that prayer? I didn't know that. I just did it because I felt led to do it, and I didn't realize the full significance of what I was doing. All over the world people are being healed. Sometimes it's months after I have prayed the prayer. Whether the engineer who makes the recording is saved or unsaved makes no difference at all. If I am anointed, the transcription carries that anointing with it. That's the thing that counts.

It's the anointing of God that heals those people in foreign lands. If I'm not anointed it isn't on the record. If I'm not anointed, it isn't in my books. People get healed reading my books. They take our magazine and lay it on their bodies as a point of contact, and get healed! Because our words have life! Because we have the Spirit of God!

I didn't realize that you could take cameras into the big tent and film the meeting and put it in a can. That's what they do with the film after they finish it; they put it into a little can, and ship it out to a TV station, and they handle it in all ways. When the anointing is captured, it transmits God into the lives of men.

I didn't know that a meeting could be filmed, and in Wichita Falls, Texas, a paralyzed girl, who had been in a wheel chair for years, would be wheeled into a room where a TV set was and 28 minutes after the TV program was put on the air, God would whisper to her, "Get out of that chair." I didn't know that until after it happened and I read the newspapers.

Take the woman with the issue of blood. She has changed the world for millions of people, and she's influencing my ministry very definitely. She proved to the world that a point of contact will release your faith. She said, "If I can touch the hem of his garment, I shall be made whole." She slipped up behind him, and when she touched his clothes with her hand, she touched him with her faith. He felt power go out of him, and said, "Who touched me?"

They said, "Why the whole crowd is jostling up against you, Jesus."

He said, "This is a different touch, for I felt the power go out of me."

She saw she was not hid, so she came up and told him what she had done. He said, "Woman, go in peace; thy faith has made thee whole."

You say, "Well if I could touch him, I would be healed." If you didn't turn your faith loose, you wouldn't. "Thy faith hath made thee whole!" She discovered the point of contact.

When I discovered the point of contact, it was the greatest discovery I ever made. Now thousands, yea, millions, of people know something about the point of contact. Our broadcast is a point of contact. TV is a point of contact. My hand is a point of contact. Our magazine, books, and laying on of hands—anything that will help people turn their faith loose—are points of contact.

Eight years ago, I came into the knowledge of a fundamental fact about God, which, before that time, was never popularized among the masses. I was sitting in Phillips University in the back row of a sociology class listening to my professor talk about human problems. The Lord spoke my name audibly, and said these words to me, "Son, don't be like other men. Don't be like other preachers. Don't be like your church. Be like Jesus! Heal the people as he healed them!"

I knew by that that I had been wrong. I had unconsciously been doing like my fellow man, my fellow preachers, and my church, which I loved so much all these years. I came then to realize that God never made the church my guide. He made Jesus the guide in my life.

I got up when the bell rang, and went out of school for the day. I said to my God, "How can I be like Jesus? I don't know how." I told the truth. It's a funny thing, but I didn't know how.

He said, "Take your Bible and read the first five books of the New Testament through consecutively three different times within one month and I will show you Jesus, and show you how to be like him."

This I did intermittently during that month. Always I read it on my knees with it spread out upon my bed, tracing the words with my finger. Within thirty days, I had read them through consecutively three times, and Jesus began to emerge. It seemed he came up out of the pages and stood up and looked me in the eye and I saw him. I saw him more clearly than most of the people who saw him with their eyes two thousand years ago.

First, God showed me that Jesus was not against any man. He wasn't against the Romans; he wasn't against the Greeks; he wasn't against the Jews. So if I would be like Jesus, I must love all races. I could not draw a color line anywhere in the world. He was not against any man. He was against only four things—sin, disease, demons, and fear. And I was to be against sin, disease, demons, and fear. I fight disease as much as I fight sin. Some people think I'm crazy. But I'm being like Jesus. I'm against sin, disease, demons, and fear, for Jesus showed me that was what he was against.

Next, I saw that he said, "I am come that they might have life, and that they might have it more abundantly." Sickness is not numbered among God's blessings. He came to give life. He didn't come to make you sick; he didn't come to make you poor; he didn't come to make you miserable; he didn't come to send you to hell. He came to give you abundant life!

I saw that, to be like Jesus, I had to offer people life. I was to preach salvation for sin, healing for disease, deliverance for demons, and a positive attitude for fear. I was to offer deliverance. I was to tell people that they could be delivered —from sin, disease, demons, and fear—and that they could be made whole, W-H-O-L-E, in body, mind, and soul. When I got hold of that knowledge I knew that I could never be the same again. I could go out and set the world on fire.

God is a good God. I coined that phrase. I said, "A God who is all this is good. God is a good God!"

Next he told me that I was to be a world missionary. The time would come when I would have to go to the ends of the earth to bring healing to my generation. He said, "Son, you are to take my healing power to your generation." I knew by that I was not to preach to a handful of people. I was not to preach to America only, but I was to make the generation conscious of divine healing. He didn't mean that everybody would accept it. He meant that I was to make the world conscious that it was available to everybody. I mean to do it. I know I can't do it alone. No man can do these things by himself. I know I have to have help. I know I have to multiply myself by the thinking of other men and women.

We are pioneering a new concept in religion. First, we are stripping from religion all of its adornments, its lost motion, its theology, its traditions of man, and we are giving the human race the *real Jesus*. We are giving people the original Jesus. I have asked my wife and my friends many times, "Why do people cry so much in our meetings?" I have looked out over my crowd and seen thousands crying. I don't tell sad stories. I just get up and preach. And people cry. I have asked many people, and every one of them gave me the same answer. They said, "Brother Roberts, you bring us Jesus!" People tell me that they see Jesus in the tent. He's the only one who can really break me up and make me cry. When I come to that pulpit, I have had a session with the Lord. I promised him I would never get into the pulpit unless I had Jesus and I could feel him when I went up there.

He told me to be like Jesus, and then he told me to give Jesus to the world. I am not trying to sell you on religion; I am not trying to sell you on my denomination; I'm trying to give you Jesus Christ. I have no axe to grind. I don't want any gift. You couldn't give me a gift privately if you had all the money in the world. I don't want anything from anybody. I want to give Jesus to the world. That is my aim in life.

Jesus said to me, "Son, you are to win one million souls to Christ in thirty-six months!" The million souls were won six and one-half months ahead of schedule. Before the last of December 1955 the last ones of the first million were saved. The television ministry changed the whole picture.

More than half of those who are saved through my ministry are being saved through the TV programs. A letter came to my desk, a part of which I want to share with you. The letter says, "Dear Brother Roberts: I'm a nurse and take care of an eighty-year-old lady in my home. The doctor came in to visit her while your TV program was on. I asked him to listen and he did. He really enjoyed the preaching. He gave his heart to God right there, and said he was glad he did."

This doctor was saved while watching the TV program. That is being done in homes all over America. TV has changed the whole picture. Jesus rode a mule. I am riding the TV receivers. Whatever is right, I will do. When they devise something more powerful, I want to use it for God.

The forces of evil are trying to shut me down. Our program has been rejected on a number of stations. We have been on certain stations for a week when they would put us off. They say that the healing line is dynamite. They say, "If you take the healing out, we will use the program." But God said, "Heal the people as Jesus healed them." So I can't take the healing line out. That is what God has told me to do—heal.

Some of the stations are plotting ways and means to break our contracts now. Our agency is doing some extracurricular work every day of the week, trying to keep us on, trying to get us on new stations. The devil is the prince of the powers of the air, and he knows what TV can do in this world if it is in the hands of God's people. It is the most powerful means the world has ever known of spreading the gospel. One woman said to me, "Brother Roberts, I have you in my front room every Sunday night." There are millions of others who have me in their front rooms. When they have me, they have somebody who will give them Jesus. It isn't a personality. It isn't just because it is I, but it is because I am giving people Jesus Christ. That is the thing that counts.

This is the opportunity of a generation. Some TV stations will not sell me time. But I haven't given up. I am determined to get on more stations. I'm going to do it some way, somehow. My partners and I may have to get together and buy out some of these stations. It takes only a change of ownership. You say, "It would cost $3,000,000 to buy a TV station." Yes, but God paves his streets with gold. He hangs up pearls for gates. His walls are solid jasper. God is not poor.

I am reaching for the world. I have introduced a novelty in my office. God told me to do it. I am bringing all races to work in my office. We are breaking the color line. All we ask is that they meet our standards. You ask anybody in my office what they are doing and they will say, "I am winning souls." We don't do a thing but win souls. One girl may type. That is true, but she is typing my answer to a letter, helping me win souls.

I have no church back of me, just the people I help. I don't write for donations. I made a rule not to do that. I am trusting God. I am believing him. My faith is in God.

This is a world organization. I am now winning souls in many foreign lands. I furnish my films free of charge to any missionary, and pay all transportation charges.

My attorney is a Jew. He said, "The thing I love about your work, Brother Roberts, is that your gospel is for all people." God so loved the world! There is nothing little about God. God is a big God, and God is a good God.

A woman who heard me preach wrote me a letter and said, "Brother Roberts, when you make plans for God, make them big." And I am. This is an outline of my program.

First, I want to get on all radio stations, not only in America but in all foreign lands where radio is in existence. I take into consideration that many foreign countries don't sell radio time, but I believe God will make a way.

Second, I am asking God to break the TV monoply against religion. I say if they sell time to the beer and cigarette interests, they ought to sell to a man of God.

I had a conference in the United States Capitol. I went into the offices of senator after senator, men whom I know personally. I went from man to man. They received me with all courtesy. I said, "Men, I ask only one thing. Tell me, is it the intent of Congress that TV shall bar religion?"

They said, "Brother Roberts, don't we have religion on TV?"

I said, "Yes, after a fashion. The TV stations choose it, and they select those who have little or no power. Healing is not allowed. The power of God is not allowed, generally speaking."

They were amazed. They promised me to go into Congress and to find the intent of the law. They are going to investigate it. I said to them, "I'm serious, don't take me lightly. I may organize a caravan and come to Washington and ask for a public hearing. We will focus the attention of all America on the fact that we can't buy time on certain TV stations."

I said, "Senators, the thing I fear is not necessarily the fact they deny me. The thing I fear is what is over the horizon. If they can deny religion time on TV at the time when we have the greatest resurgence of faith our country has ever known, if in this revival they can get by with saying no, what will they do when the revival spirit is over? We must break the monopoly now."

Think of your own children. If the TV stations can shut their doors in our face in this great spiritual revival, what about thirty years from now when no man knows what may happen? The battle we are fighting is for the gospel and to win the souls of men. TV is a soul winner when the anointing is on it.

In my meeting in Johannesburg in January of 1955, twenty thousand souls were won to Christ in eight days among the whites and ten thousand among the blacks. Then I organized a 100,000 Souls Crusade in South Africa. With the money I raised (which I couldn't bring back to America) I am financing native preachers. One of them had a campaign recently and won six thousand souls in one campaign. I am counting these souls in my Million Souls Crusade. The churches give the men. I support those men and they preach a message that has life in it.

Similar committees will be organized in the Philippines and Australia, because the money I raise there can't be brought back. So I will leave it to work for souls and count them in our Million Souls Crusade.

Then, I plan to print picture books about Jesus—books for the children of this wicked world. I will be the first to do this on a large scale—a million at a time. We are now preparing a new cartoon book that presents the gospel in pictures. Most folks will look at a picture when they won't read. I am preparing this in the languages and for the different nationalities of the world, using the same pictures. The first printing of a million copies will be ready soon. I am in a crusade to print the gospel. Don't underestimate the power of the printed word.

I am going to preach to the Indians. I have an entree among Indians that no other preacher in America has. They love me. My name is a household word among the reservations. The attention of America will focus upon the Indians of this country.

The biggest part of my program is the Jewish project. I feel that the success or failure of my ministry hinges on the Jewish work. There is no revival in Israel. There is no revival among the Jews. The time has come for it, but it hasn't happened. They don't have the Holy Bible and they are not being preached to. "How can they hear without a preacher?" Now I am printing the Bible in Hebrew with an insert proving by the Scriptures that Jesus is the Christ. I am distributing these Hebrew Bibles among the Jews of the world, but principally in Israel. Dr. Myron Sackett has joined forces with us. Brother Lester Sumrall is going to set up our national headquarters in Jerusalem. He's going there to get workers and to get these Bibles out. He will preach and prepare the way for me to go hold a meeting. Faith cometh by hearing. You can't discount the Word of God. The first step is to put the Bible in their hands. If we will bless the Jews, God will bless us; but if we curse them, we will be cursed. The Bible says it. History proves it. They are wonderful people and I love them. I love them and I make no apology for it.

There is an urgency in me that burns me up. I have a fire burning in me so strongly that I can hardly stand it. There is a voice that screams in my ear, "Now, now, now!" I hear it day and night. This is God's work, and I can't rest. The world is waiting to be changed by the power of God.

Jesus, a Mighty Saviour

5

. . . Joseph, thou son of David, fear not to take unto thee Mary thy wife: for that which is conceived in her is of the Holy Ghost. And she shall bring forth a son, and thou shalt call his name JESUS: for he shall save his people from their sins (MATTHEW 1:20,21).

It is a fascinating thing to learn how Jesus was named, how he got the name *Jesus.*

The mighty archangel Gabriel named the child Jesus. And the name that Gabriel gave him was perhaps one thing that convinced Joseph that he should marry Mary.

Mary, you know, was the fiancée of Joseph. They were not yet married when he discovered that this girl was with child. He was a just man, and he didn't want to expose her publicly, so he privately set about to break the engagement. One night he was asleep and Gabriel awakened him and said to him, "Joseph, thou son of David, fear not to take unto thee Mary thy wife: for that which is conceived in her is of the Holy Ghost. And she shall bring forth a son, and thou shalt call his name JESUS: for he shall save his people from their sins." When Joseph realized what a great child this was to be, he went ahead and married the girl and became the foster father of Jesus.

The thing we are interested in now is the name *Jesus*. It literally means Saviour. He was sent into the world to save the human family. When I was in the Holy Land a few months ago, in Nazareth and in Bethany, it seemed to me that the name Gabriel gave him rang in my ears. I was always conscious of the name *Jesus*. In fact, Jesus is more important to me than my wife is, or my children are, or anybody else in this whole world. I love Jesus more than I love my wife, and she knows it and she is not jealous. Loving him more than I love her does not diminish my love for her, because the more you love Jesus, the more you can love other people. One woman said to me, "Brother Roberts, I think I love my children too much."

I said, "Oh, no, you just don't love the Lord enough. If you love Jesus enough, you can't love people too much, for he died for every one of us."

Joseph seemed to catch the significance of the name *Jesus*, for he did something that not many men would do in any generation—he actually married the girl who was carrying a child before wedlock. It was a strange thing, the way the Holy Spirit came upon that girl and conceived in her womb the holy child Jesus. You might imagine the public ridicule to which she and Joseph would be exposed. But he took the woman to be his wife and knew her not until the child was born, because he realized the name *Jesus* held in it the magic power to save the human race.

JESUS IS A MIGHTY SAVIOUR

First, he is a mighty Saviour from sin, that evil monster from which springs the unholy trinity of sickness, fear, and demons. Sin is the monster that destroys. It is the evil power that separates the person from the Creator. It is that evil, destroying power that blasts our characters, damns our souls, lowers our appetites, and makes us lower than the animals of the field. Sin is that awful power that brings hate into our hearts, revenge into our minds; it is the awful thing that fills us with inner conflicts and frustrations and torments and fears. It is the power that turns us against God and against our fellow man, that makes us hate ourselves. It is that power which destroys other people, and destroys us, that sends us to hell. Jesus is a mighty Saviour from the power of sin.

For instance, Jesus saves people that nobody else will look at. Jesus picks up people who have fallen so low that not even the devil will speak to them any more. You take the woman in the Bible who was caught in the act of adultery. The religious people caught her for one reason only—to cast her out of the church. They didn't catch her to save her: they caught her to excommunicate her. They brought her to Christ and said, "What would you do to this woman?"

Jesus stooped and wrote on the ground and said to her accusers, "Which of you is not guilty?" They all slunk away.

Then he said, "Woman, where art thine accusers?"

She said, "I know not, Lord."

He said, "Woman, I don't condemn you either. Go and sin no more." She picked herself off the ground and stood up, a woman saved by Jesus, good enough for the arms of any man, clean as God can make a human, good enough to be the mother of anybody ever born. That's what Jesus does for sinners.

The other night I boarded a plane for home. There was a vacant seat on my right, and as I took it I noticed I was sitting by a woman approaching fifty years of age. When I sat down, I introduced myself and she said, "Oh, I've been wanting to meet you. I have something I must ask you."

She opened her heart and told me her story. She had been recently divorced, and was in love with a married man, and she was in trouble. She said to me, "Will God save me?"

The sin of adultery is probably the most prevalent sin of our time. It is catching more people than any other sin. Those people are human beings; they have been created by God. We don't like what they do and they don't like it either, but they're caught in it and they need a Saviour. They have one—Jesus of Nazareth.

The woman on the plane said to me, "Brother Roberts, I trust you, or I wouldn't tell you this." She began to stumble and falter as she tried to tell me, but I was ahead of her. I felt it. I discerned her trouble as I sat there, and I said, "I don't know what you are expecting of me, but you need not expect me to condemn you, because I don't. I don't condemn anybody for anything they do. I'll just tell you now, there's One who can save you as you sit here on this plane."

She said, "Mr. Roberts, do you believe I can be saved *right now?*"

I said, "Yes, *right now.*"

I had the funniest feeling in the world. There I was, high up in the air, sitting by a woman who was like the woman in the Bible, who wanted me to help her get saved. I said, "Well, if you were in my big tent, I would know how to help you get saved. I would have you in the healing line or you could come forward during the altar call and repeat the sinner's prayer."

"Well," she said, "I want to be saved. I've never been saved in my life. I've been a member of a church for all these years; I am now, but I'm not saved."

I said, "Give me your hand."

I had her repeat the sinner's prayer after me, and asked God to save her. I felt God's power go through my hand. Then I stopped praying and looked at her. I said, "You know, I forgot to tell you that when the Lord's power comes upon me, I usually feel it in my right hand."

She said, "Well, you didn't need to tell me. I felt the power of God going into me." She said she had never felt the power of God in her whole life before, but she was wonderfully saved there on the plane.

Now that's Jesus. That's the kind of Jesus I believe in. He *is* a mighty Saviour.

Second, he is a mighty Saviour from fear. God said to his Son, "Go down, Jesus, into the earth and save my people from their fears."

There was a little baby born some six months before Jesus was, and his name was John the Baptist. He grew up and became the forerunner of Christ. You know, he is the one who preached and announced Jesus was in the world, and said, "Behold the Lamb of God which taketh away the sin of the world." John the Baptist was a great man, but he was only the forerunner of the real Jesus.

When John the Baptist was born, the Spirit of God came upon his father, Zacharias, and he gave one of the most beautiful prophecies recorded in the Bible. He told how God was visiting his people. He said, "God will deliver us from our enemies, that we may serve him without fear all the days of our lives." Through Jesus people can live without fear. Nobody can take fear from you and keep you free from it, and enable you to live totally without fear, except Jesus. He is a mighty Saviour from fear.

A woman came into my meeting in a wheel chair. They put her in the invalid room. When I walked up to her, she grabbed my hands and said, "Brother Roberts, look at me." Her face was etched with the lines of suffering and her hands were knotted with arthritis. She said, "Brother Roberts, six months ago I was a well and normal woman, and tonight I cannot walk." She said, "This is what my fears did to me." I was delighted to present to her Jesus, the mighty Saviour from fear. That woman was healed. She came out of the wheel chair. She is healed now, as far as I know. But how was she healed? She was healed first, by believing Jesus to take fear out of her mind. Jesus can take fear away from you. People who are insane are brought through my line. Many of them are insane because of their fears. In a previous meeting, I had a group of little children brought to me who were scared. They were so full of fear that they weren't normal. The parents begged me to pray for them because they were constantly afraid. It was my joy to pray for those people and see them healed, because Christ is a mighty Saviour from fear.

Third, he is a mighty Saviour from demons. Demons are evil spirits that do not have a body. They once had a body, when they were angels in the presence of God, and their leader, Lucifer, was an archangel. But he rebelled against God and sinned, and God cast him out of Heaven with one-third of the angels, and they lost their celestial bodies. They were cast down to the earth, and Lucifer is now the devil. He is a fallen archangel. These angels who fell with him lost their celestial bodies, and now they are called demons. The word *demon* means *tormentor.* In the Gospel of Matthew, Chapter 12, Jesus refers to them as "walking about in dry places, seeking rest and finding none." These evil spirits seek people, because, since they lost their bodies, they are almost powerless. When they enter into a human and possess him, they have a human body, a human mind, and a human spirit. They make the person what they are. Whatever the demon is, the person becomes. When a demon enters a person, that person takes on the characteristics of that particular demon. If it's an unclean demon, the person becomes unclean.

There are many forms of demons: demons that derange the mind, demons that possess the soul, demons that enter the body and cause certain kinds of diseases. In the Book of Luke we are told that Christ healed a woman of a *spirit of infirmity* which had bound that woman until she was as stiff as a board. Christ called out the spirit of infirmity and she was healed. Once in possession of a human body, these demon spirits have terrible power. People who live in sin are open to demon power. There are millions of demons. They cannot be seen with the eye, but they work where Christ is not. They have no power where Christ is, for Christ came in the power of the Spirit of God and had absolute power to cast them out. The thing the devil hated most was Christ's power over demons. And this power Jesus gave to his disciples. He gave them power over all unclean spirits and to cast them out. This is the power that Christ gave me in 1947. He said, "Son, from this hour you will heal the sick and cast out devils by my power." From that time I have probably, by the Spirit of God, cast out more demons than any man alive today. We have had thousands of cases. They are taken to the invalid room, because some of them are too violent to be put out in public. When the conditions are right, when we believe like we should, we are always successful. But many things enter into it, and there is so little knowledge about demons. We need to read the Bible and think along these lines. The more God's people take the authority Christ has given them, the more successful we will be among these unfortunate people.

Christ has given us four powers: First, the power to discern demons; second, the power to cast them out; third, the power to forbid their re-entering the person; and fourth, the power to keep them from entering us. When the blood of Christ is on your soul and you are saved by that blood, no demon can cross the blood line of Christ. You are as safe as Christ is safe, for no demon has control over Jesus. He is a mighty Saviour from demon power.

Fourth, he is a mighty Saviour from disease. He said, "Heal the sick, cleanse the lepers, raise the dead, cast out devils: freely ye have received, freely give" (Matthew 10:8). Matthew 8:17 reminds us that "Himself took our infirmities, and bare our sicknesses." The stripes upon Jesus' back are for the healing of our diseases. I stood in an underground chamber in Jerusalem many feet below the level of the streets. I stood under the Roman arches of the road along which Christ passed, and I stood in the exact spot where the soldier of Rome took the scourge of the whip and striped the body of Jesus. As I stood there in that place, I literally envisioned what was going on. They took Christ and stripped his body, tied his wrists to a peg in the wall above his head, and the Roman soldier took the whip of leather, which was loaded with bits of brass to lacerate the flesh. As I stood there, I heard, in my mind, what was going on. *Lash! Lash! Lash! Lash!* There is a healing stripe for every disease.

Jesus gave power to his disciples to heal. Acts 10:38 says he went about doing good. "God anointed Jesus of Nazareth with the Holy Ghost and with power: who went about doing good, and healing all that were oppressed of the devil; for God was with him." Now Jesus is a mighty Saviour from sickness. "The prayer of faith shall save the sick, and the Lord shall raise them up . . ." (James 5:15). Who shall raise them up? The *Lord* shall raise them up! *Jesus* shall raise them up! *Jesus* can save your body from its sickness. *Jesus* can destroy the sickness in your body! *Jesus* is a mighty Saviour from sickness and disease! Do you believe it?

The little woman in the Bible with the issue of blood said, "If I may but touch his garment, I shall be whole." She touched his clothes with her hand and believed. Immediately healing power went out of him and he said, "Who touched me?"

The crowd said, "Everybody is jostling up against you."

He said, "This was a different touch, for I felt healing virtue go out of me." The woman knew that she was not hidden. She ran up and said, "Lord, I touched you."

He said, "Daughter, be of good comfort; thy faith hath made thee whole."

I brought you this story for this reason, to let you know that *Jesus* is actually full of healing virtue. The Man is brimful of healing power, and to touch him is to be healed. To have him touch you is to be healed. Jesus is a mighty Saviour from sickness and disease.

I pray for thousands of people to be healed and whenever I can get Oral Roberts in harmony with Jesus and get the people in harmony with Jesus, Jesus becomes our mighty Saviour today to heal the sicknesses and diseases of our bodies. I've been healed by Jesus. I was healed of a stuttering tongue and tuberculosis in both lungs. It is very wonderful to have a good, strong body, to have your mind clean and strong, and to know that your soul is saved by the blood of Christ. You are not afraid and you know that no demon can enter your life. I don't know anything in the world as wonderful as to be saved by Jesus. *Jesus—Jesus!* Jesus is the sweetest name I know.

Jesus is the sweetest name I know,
And he's just the same as his lovely name.
That's the reason why I love him so,
For Jesus is the sweetest name I know.

God Is Not a Man

6

I had never thought of it before.

It had not dawned on me.

I guess I knew it, but I had not grasped its full significance.

I remember my feeling when I first discovered it.

I was reading the twenty-third chapter of the Book of Numbers.

I came to the nineteenth verse and stopped. *God is not a man, that he should lie; neither the son of man, that he should repent: hath he said, and shall he not do it? or hath he spoken, and shall he not make it good?* (Num. 23:19).

This verse was the climax of a powerful sermon preached by the prophet Balaam to Balak, a wicked king.

The prophet said, "God is not a man."

A feeling of vast relief flooded my soul.

"Thank God," I said, "God is not a man."

Balaam's pronouncement gave meaning and power to something I already knew and believed.

What has this got to do with your deliverance from sickness or fear or any other torment of your life?

Knowing God is not a man can mean everything.

We rub elbows every day with failure.

We are circumscribed by our physical limitations.

Nature's hands can reach only so far.

Medicine can do only so much.

The best doctor, by his own admission, is limited.

We must never confuse God with man.

God is not limited.

God is all-power.

God is all-wise.

God is everywhere present at the same time.

"For with God," the angel said, "nothing shall be impossible" (Luke 1:37).

Balaam, the prophet of God, learned this in a striking, dramatic fashion.

Israel came marching behind Moses from Egypt, across the Red Sea, and through desert plain, on their way to Canaan—the land flowing with milk and honey.

They were singing, shouting, and praising God.

No man, no nation, no earthly power could stand before them.

Balak, King of Moab, saw them coming, and a terrible hatred against God's anointed came into his heart. He threw all the power of his armies against them but nothing he did prospered against them. A cunning plan came into his mind. He attempted to bribe Balaam to curse these people. The prophet's eyes were blinded by this bribe, and he went forth to curse Israel in the name of the Lord. He did not see the angel of God who was standing before him with a drawn sword in his hand. But the mule on which he was riding saw the angel and became frightened. Three times the mule saw the angel and the third time he fell down on Balaam and the prophet began to smite him. God gave the animal the power of human speech. "Balaam, why are you smiting me?" cried the mule. "Because you have mocked me these three times," answered Balaam. The angel opened Balaam's eyes. The prophet saw the angel with the drawn sword and he fell down before him. The angel told him to get up and go on top of the mountain and behold the people of God in their glory and power. Balaam saw these people. He heard the shout of a king among them. Then God spoke to him and told him to go back and answer King Balak. Later, the king asked him what the Lord had said. Balaam answered, "Behold, I have received commandment to bless and he hath blessed and I cannot reverse it." Balak said, "Neither curse them at all nor bless them." Balaam answered, "All that the Lord speaketh, that I must do."

GOD CANNOT LIE

Lying is a characteristic of man, not of God.

This is one of the great things about God—he cannot lie.

There is no lying in his nature.

God had appeared to Moses in a burning bush while Moses was in the backside of a desert. Moses was a runaway and a failure.

When he turned aside to see the bush, God said, "Moses!"

Moses said, "Here am I."

God told him to take off his shoes for he was standing on holy ground.

Then the Lord said, "I have surely seen the affliction of my people which are in Egypt and have heard their cry by reason of their taskmasters. I know their sorrows. Come now, therefore, and I will send thee unto Pharaoh and thou shalt bring forth my people, the children of Israel, out of Egypt."

Moses said unto God, "Who am I that I should go unto Pharaoh and that I should bring forth the children of Israel out of Egypt?"

God said, "I will be with thee. I will stretch out my hand and smite Egypt with all my wonders and he will let you go. I will bring you up out of the afflictions of Egypt unto the land of Canaan into a land flowing with milk and honey."

There in the limitless desert, God spoke to Moses and gave him his solemn word that he would deliver his people and establish them in the land of Canaan.

Balak had bribed Balaam the prophet to get God to break his word and curse his anointed.

God told Balaam to tell Balak that God is not a man that he would lie.

We live in a world of lies. Man has broken his word so often it is difficult for him to believe any more.

It is good to know that God is not a man. He cannot lie.

Take the Bible and hold it in your hand a few moments. Look at it. Leaf through a few of its pages. Think how old it is, how permanent, how changeless. It is the same Bible your grandfather and father read. It is the same Bible your children will read. Your grandchildren will study it. That Bible you hold in your hand says, "God cannot lie." Sometimes when I am under great stress, going through some terrible trial, have some problem that baffles me, am misunderstood, am severely criticized, and desperately need help, I take my Bible to bed with me, and sleep with it in the cradle of my arms. It reminds me that God cannot lie. God will deliver me. God is not a man. The devil's kingdom is built on a lie. Therefore, it will fall. God has built his kingdom on truth, and it will last forever. What God was in Moses' day, he is in our day. He delivered his people then. He will deliver his people now. The Scriptures say that Jesus Christ is the same yesterday, today, and forever.

This was something else that Balaam learned about God. "I have received commandment to bless and not curse," Balaam said, "and I cannot reverse it."

GOD IS TOTALLY GOOD

God is not a man; therefore, he is totally good.

It was a great day in my life when I discovered the total goodness of God. I was hurrying out of the house to catch a bus for an early morning class at the university. I suddenly remembered I had not read anything in the Bible. I ran back, grabbed up my Bible, opened it at random, and began to read.

The little book of 3 John was the one I began to read. When I came to the second verse, I stopped: "Beloved, I wish above all things that thou mayest prosper and be in health, even as thy soul prospereth." This verse fascinated me. It got hold of me. It opened up a new world for me. After that I didn't care whether I made my class or not.

When I discovered this powerful verse in the Bible, it changed my life. I sat there with my Bible in my hand and, for the first time in my life, I knew that God was totally good.

Where the phrase came from I perhaps will never know, but out of my spirit came this statement which I have said thousands of times across America: *God is a good God, and the devil is a bad devil.*

God is good, totally good, always and forever good, and he will never reverse his nature. Other Scriptures substantiate this great thought.

Take Paul's statement for instance. "Christ hath redeemed us from the curse of the law, being made a curse for us: for it is written, Cursed is every one that hangeth on a tree" (Galatians 3:13).

Take John's statement. "The thief cometh not, but for to steal, and to kill, and to destroy: I am come that they might have life, and that they might have it more abundantly" (John 10:10).

Take Peter's statement. "God anointed Jesus of Nazareth with the Holy Ghost and with power: who went about doing good, and healing all that were oppressed of the devil; for God was with him" (Acts 10:38).

In Luke 9:56, Jesus said, "The Son of man is not come to destroy men's lives, but to save them."

According to Jesus, your afflictions, your torments, and your troubles come from the devil.

Jesus said that the thief (which is the devil) cometh not, but for to steal, to kill, and to destroy.

Peter said that Jesus was anointed by the Holy Ghost to heal all who are oppressed of the devil.

Jesus said that he came to give men life and to give it to them more abundantly.

Jesus said he did not come to destroy people but to save them.

It is Satan's will that you be sick.

It is God's will that you be well.

It is Satan's will that you be poverty-stricken.

It is God's will that you prosper.

It is Satan's will that you be afraid.

It is God's will that you believe and live without fear.

It is Satan's will that you live a defeated, miserable life.

It is God's will that you be more than a conqueror through Christ who loves you and died for you.

There is no goodness in the devil, and no badness in God.

The devil is totally bad, and God is totally good.

When you become sick, don't say, "God made me sick."

When you are afraid, don't say, "God has made me afraid."

When you cannot meet your obligations, do not say, "God wants me to be poor."

When you are defeated, do not say, "God wants me to be miserable."

Don't forget 3 John 2. "Beloved, I wish above all things that thou mayest prosper and be in health, even as thy soul prospereth."

THREE ATTRIBUTES OF GOD

God is not a man; therefore he has three attributes that man does not have.

God is omnipotent, omnipresent, and omniscient.

God is omnipotent. This means he is all-powerful.

God is omnipresent. This means he is everywhere present at the same time.

He is omniscient. This means he is all-wise.

A young smart aleck, who had just graduated from college, said to his old dad: "Father, where is God?"

"Son, where is he not?" the father replied.

About three years ago this attribute of God saved my family.

There was a noise at the back door. Somebody was trying to break down the door. Evelyn woke up in a panic. The children were asleep in an adjoining room. The lady who had been staying with my family was not there that night. Sitting on the side of the bed, Evelyn was trembling. She was so paralyzed with fear that she couldn't think what she should do. Suddenly the noise stopped. Evelyn found herself relaxed and no longer afraid. A great peace and calmness came over her. She was able to lie down and go back to sleep.

I was 1,400 miles away in Norfolk, Virginia, while this was going on in my home in Tulsa, Oklahoma. Something woke me out of a sound sleep. I had the uncanny feeling that someone was in my room. I jumped out of bed, turned on the light, and searched the room. I started to get back in bed when almost literally I saw Evelyn and my children in terrible danger. I saw them almost as plainly as if I were there in person. I have never seen an angel, but I was certain an angel was there in the room with me. I fell on my knees and asked God to protect my family. In a few minutes I felt light all over and knew that God was undertaking. I was able to go back to bed and sleep the rest of the night.

After the Norfolk campaign was over, I flew home. I had not been in the house over thirty minutes when Evelyn said, "Oral, I had a bad scare while you were gone this time." I said, "What happened?"

Then she told me about it.

She said, "I was so scared that I was almost paralyzed. I knew if I called the police they wouldn't have time to get here. I didn't want to wake the children because I knew they would be afraid."

"What did you do?"

"That is the funny part. I didn't do anything. All of a sudden I was not afraid. The noise stopped and I felt everything was all right. I went back to sleep."

I asked her what night it was and what time of the night. She told me.

It was the same night and the same hour of the night when God's angel had awakened me in my room and shown me they were in danger.

God was with me in Norfolk, Virginia, and he was with my wife in Tulsa, 1,400 miles away.

God is all-wise, and he let me know that they needed my

prayers. God is omnipresent. He is everywhere at the same time. He was there with me in Norfolk and there with my wife Evelyn in Tulsa. God is omnipotent. His great power came to me. His great power came to Evelyn. His great power drove the intruder away.

GOD IS ABOVE NATURE

God is not a man; therefore, he is not subject to the laws of nature.

It is contrary to the laws of nature for the sun to stand still.

When Joshua and the children of Israel were fighting the battle of the Lord, Joshua saw that if he had a little more time he would win complete victory.

The sun was going down when suddenly Joshua raised his right hand and spoke, "Sun, stand thou still."

The sun hung like a mirror in the sky.

It is contrary to the laws of nature for time to run backwards.

Hezekiah, the King of Israel, was sick and the prophet Isaiah came and told him to put his house in order for he was going to die. Hezekiah turned his face toward the wall and wept and prayed before God.

The Lord told him he would heal him.

Isaiah gave him a choice of a point of contact.

The king said to Isaiah, "What shall be the sign that the Lord will heal me?"

Isaiah said, "This sign shalt thou have of the Lord, that the Lord will do the thing that he hath spoken: shall the shadow go forward ten degrees, or go back ten degrees?"

Hezekiah answered, "It is a light thing for the shadow to go down ten degrees: nay, but let the shadow return backward ten degrees."

Isaiah cried unto the Lord and he brought the shadow ten degrees backward, by which it had gone down in the dial of Ahaz.

Through this sign as a point of contact, Hezekiah believed and was healed.

As a sign, and to answer Hezekiah's point of contact for the release of his faith, God made time go in reverse.

For 40 minutes, everything not only stood still, but went backward.

The sun went back; the moon went back; the stars went back; the earth went back. Everything went backwards on its course for 40 minutes. It is contrary to the laws of nature for time to run backwards. But God is not a man; therefore, he is not subject to the laws of nature.

It is contrary to the laws of nature for ravens to feed a man, but ravens fed the prophet Elijah.

The prophet had issued his ultimatum to King Ahab that there would be no rain upon the earth until his word. Elijah fled and for a time lived in a cave. When his food ran out God commanded the ravens to feed him.

Ravens are black and are symbols of death. Edgar Allan Poe, one of the great poets of this country, made *The Raven* the title of one of his most famous poems. In this poem, Edgar Allan Poe uses the raven as a symbol of his bondage to liquor, dope, frustration, and utter defeat. Everyone who has ever read *The Raven* knows how Edgar Allan Poe looked upon the raven as a symbol of death and defeat.

God commanded the black-winged ravens, symbols of death, to become his instruments and feed his prophet. The ravens brought him bread and flesh in the morning and bread and flesh in the evening, and the prophet's life was sustained.

It is contrary to the laws of nature for a man to walk on water.

When Jesus said, "Come," Peter leaped out of the boat and walked on the water to go to Jesus.

It is contrary to the laws of nature for a fish to pay one's taxes.

When Jesus and the disciples' taxes were due, the Lord said to Peter, "Go cast your hook into the sea and the first fish you catch will be the banker of the lot."

Peter went down to the seashore, threw in his hook, and soon he yanked in a big fish, hand over fist.

He opened its mouth, pulled out the bank roll and paid his and the Lord's taxes.

It is contrary to the laws of nature for faith to heal an organic disease.

The little woman in the Bible who had an issue of blood said, "If I can touch only the hem of his garment, I shall be made whole." She came to the outskirts of the crowd and saw she would have no way of talking with Jesus. She made her way through the great audience and reached down and touched the hem of his garment as he was walking away. Instantly her issue of blood stopped and she was healed. Jesus said, "Who touched me?" The disciples said, "Lord, everybody is touching you and jostling up against you." Jesus said, "This was a different touch." When she touched his clothes with her hand, she touched him with her faith. She was instantly healed.

Yes, friend, it may be contrary to the laws of nature that you be healed of your diseases. But God is not a man; therefore, he is not subject to the laws of nature.

You may think it isn't possible that your financial needs will be met.

It may seem impossible to you that your life will ever amount to anything.

Your afflictions may be incurable to man.

But God is not a man. He is not subject to the laws of nature.

Turn your thinking and believing toward him. He can help you. He can deliver you. He can make you whole.

Remember, he is not a man.

He cannot lie.

He is totally good.

He is omnipotent, omniscient, omnipresent.

He is not subject to the laws of nature.

Accept this as I have done. Believe in him and turn your faith loose and he will do great things for you.

7 There Is No Distance in Prayer

Whither shall I go from thy spirit? or whither shall I flee from thy presence? If I ascend up into heaven, thou art there: if I make my bed in hell, behold, thou art there. If I take the wings of the morning, and dwell in the uttermost parts of the sea; even there shall thy hand lead me, and thy right hand shall hold me (PSALM 139:7–10).

God is in this place where I am. He is there in that place with you. He is here and he is there. He is exactly where I am, and he is a thousand miles from this exact spot. He is ten thousand miles out there, for God is omnipresent.

Since God is everywhere, faith, wherever it goes into operation or wherever it is released, works. It moves God here where I am and there where you are. I believe here and he works there, performing the miracle of deliverance where it is needed.

Recently I made a program here in Tulsa, preaching a sermon on deliverance and praying the healing prayer. God anointed me, and when this program was put on the air on hundreds of stations here in America and several powerful stations in many foreign lands, the anointing carried through to the listeners. Naturally, the program was in English. A woman seriously ill in Norway heard my voice over Radio Luxembourg, the most powerful station in Europe. She couldn't understand a word of English. Two words stuck in her mind: my name, Oral Roberts. However, she later testified that there was power in my voice. Suddenly she sensed I was praying. She felt impelled to rush over to her radio and place her hands on it. As my voice continued to utter the healing prayer she felt the surging of God's power enter her body, and in the flash of a second she was healed!

Chaplain Jake Till of the U.S. Air Force, who showed our film in England and on the Continent while he was off duty, was recently visiting in Norway. This woman was conversing with him through an interpreter. She heard him mention my name. Her face lit up. "Oral Roberts? Do you know him?"

"Yes, I know him," Chaplain Till replied. "He is on Radio Luxembourg with his healing broadcast each week."

Then she told him the above story of how she was healed. I prayed in Tulsa, Oklahoma. This prayer was put on Radio Luxembourg in Europe. A woman in Norway, who couldn't understand a word I was saying, felt God's power in my voice and was instantly and completely healed.

There is no distance in prayer. God was with me in Tulsa when I prayed, was in Luxembourg in Europe when the program was released, and was in Norway with the woman who couldn't understand English. God is everywhere; therefore, there is no distance in prayer.

A high church official in South Africa heard my voice on

our broadcast over Radio Lourenço Marques, and he was healed of an incurable kidney disease. He immediately became one of the instruments to take me to South Africa in my first missionary campaign in foreign lands. There is no distance in prayer.

The Bible was written thousands of years ago, in different places on the earth by different men, all of whom were moved by the Holy Spirit of God. The words of these writers are put together on today's printing presses, bound in one volume, and sold to us in the bookstores. We open that book and read the words which God had men write. Together, they make up the Word of God—the Book of Life. Widely separated from the time and place it was written, it has the same effect upon us today as it did the day it was first revealed, because there is no distance in prayer. Believe the Bible today and God will deliver you completely—in soul, mind, and body.

A woman in England received a copy of our magazine, HEALING, and was reading the middle spread of healing testimonies. Suddenly, she felt an urge to make the magazine her point of contact. She placed the magazine upon her afflicted body. Standing there, she said, "This magazine has in it the words of life from a man you have called to heal the sick. Heal me, Lord, and make me whole." She testified that God's power swept through her like liquid fire and she experienced perfect healing.

GOD GAVE US JESUS

God loves people. He wants to be near us. He gave us Jesus to speak with us face to face, to touch us with his hands and heal us, to bless us and give us his power. That is why he sent Jesus, who got just as close to people as he could with his hands, his voice, and his robe. Then he died for people, rose again, ascended back to Heaven, interceded for them, gave gifts to them, and promised to come for them.

One thing Jesus made clear—*there is no distance in prayer.* Jesus' hands laid upon the sick were powerful to heal, but his spoken word was just as powerful as the touch of his hands. He could heal in person and he could heal at a distance.

Jesus healed the centurion's servant at a distance, by using his voice only. That's all the centurion asked for—Jesus' voice. Jesus was willing to go to the bedside of the servant and heal him. But the centurion said, "Speak the word only, Lord, and my servant shall be healed." Jesus spoke and the "servant was healed in the selfsame hour" (Matthew 8:13).

There is no distance in prayer, because faith bridges the distance and brings near those things which are faraway. God, who is everywhere, does the healing. The thing that counts is not nearness or distance but our believing!

Jesus raised Lazarus from the dead, not by putting his hands upon him but by speaking the word. Lazarus lay thirty-five steps down in the bottom of the grave. He had four days of death in his body, and was bound hand and foot with graveclothes. Jesus spoke in a loud voice: "Lazarus, come forth" (John 11:43). The dead heard the voice of the Lord of Life. Jesus' voice pulled Lazarus up the thirty-five steps and restored him to his sisters, Mary and Martha.

When Legion, bound by demons, came rushing down the hill toward Jesus and the disciples as they came ashore on Gadara, Jesus called the demons out and healed him by his voice only. "Thou unclean spirits, come out!" Jesus cried, and Legion was loosed and set free (Mark 5:8–13).

In one of our recent campaigns, I was praying for the sick in the healing line when suddenly I sensed that great faith was present among the huge audience. I stopped and told them I was going to use my voice as a point of contact for their healing. I would not lay my hands upon them, for they had faith to be healed without the touch of my hands. I lifted my voice and prayed the healing prayer. They heard my voice only. My spoken word was just as powerful as the laying on of my hands. Over one thousand people, by actual count, leaped to their feet, crowded into the aisles, and testified that they had been instantly healed.

PERSONAL SYMBOLS

There is no distance in prayer. The thing that counts is faith. Since this is true, the symbols of one's personal presence are just as powerful as the spoken word or the laying on of the hands.

When Paul had laid his hands upon as many as he could, when he had spoken to as many as he could, then he healed at a distance through symbols of his personal presence.

"Take this handkerchief from my pocket and the apron (outer garment) from my body," he said, "and lay upon the sick and the demon-possessed. Let this handkerchief or this apron be as though Paul stood there" (paraphrased from Acts 19:11,12). Special miracles were wrought this way upon both the sick and those possessed with demons. The thing that counted was Paul's faith. When he believed, there was no distance in prayer.

I sent a small square of cloth to a mother for the healing of her baby. "Let it be as if I stood over your baby in prayer," I wrote. Her child was miraculously healed!

There is no distance in prayer, if we believe.

Take the Communion of the Lord's Supper. If we can believe, the broken bread becomes Jesus' body and the wine becomes his blood. There is healing in the Communion when we believe. Our believing transports us directly to Jesus, for he is everywhere present at the same time. The emblems of bread and wine are as though Jesus stood directly by us.

The next time you take the Lord's Supper, remember this.

Peter's shadow, a symbol of his personal presence, was used to bring healing to the multitudes of sick folk in Jerusalem: "Let the shadow of my body falling upon you be as my voice or as my hands upon you" (paraphrased from Acts 5:15,16).

MY PERSONAL LETTERS

When I write you a personal letter offering prayer for you, let my written word be as if I personally stood there. When you get a prayer cloth from me, let it be as though I personally stood there. When you read these words from my pen, let it be as though I stood there. When you hear my voice on the radio, let it be as though I stood there. When you see me on television and I reach forth my hand to pray for you, let it be as though I stood in the room with you.

BIBLE REASONS

Why is there no distance in prayer? Why is it that our believing counts so much? For these three Bible reasons:

(1) Believing recognizes God's power and authority anywhere and everywhere (Matthew 8:5–13).

(2) Believing has complete mastery over all our torments and ills (Matthew 8:13; Mark 9:23).

(3) These things—the laying on of hands, the spoken word, handkerchiefs, or prayer cloths, etc.—are points of contact for the release of your faith. It is faith that delivers.

There is a special intimacy between God and the one who

believes in him. There is also an intimacy among those true Christians who believe alike, who have the same kind of faith, who love alike.

How often we feel God. How often we feel each other. There is distance between us only physically. Spiritually, we are very near to each other.

So many write, "Brother Roberts, last Sunday on your broadcast it seemed you were sitting right beside me, and I get the same feeling when I read your books or your articles in the magazine."

Why do these people feel my nearness? Because I am near them. God has put a touch of himself in my soul, and I feel, in some inexplainable way, those to whom I minister. My mind leaps across the barriers of physical limitations and becomes one with theirs.

How many times I have felt the prayer of those who pray for me. Sometimes I am so acutely aware of prayer for me that I feel a new surge of power, a quickening of my faith, a greater intensity of burden for lost souls. *Truly there is no distance in prayer.*

8 Get off the Briar and Get on the Wing —As the Eagle Stirreth Up Her Nest

Here is a great sermon just as it was preached in the big tent cathedral, tape-recorded and typed for publication. To thousands of our readers, who have attended Oral Roberts' campaigns, the tent atmosphere in this sermon will be so real as to bring back to them the odor of sawdust.—G. H. M.

Ye have seen what I did unto the Egyptians, and how I bare you on eagles' wings, and brought you unto myself (EXODUS 19:4).

As an eagle stirreth up her nest, fluttereth over her young, spreadeth abroad her wings, taketh them, beareth them on her wings: so the Lord alone did lead him (DEUTERONOMY 32:11,12).

I wish to speak to you on eagles or God's way of dealing with humanity. The eagle has a strong and powerful wing. She builds her nest on high places, in high trees or on high, rocky ledges. She builds her nest with sticks and briars and she covers it with rags, skins of animals, and soft, downy feathers. The eagle hatches her eggs and brings up her little ones in this nest. The eagle is a wonderful mother. The Bible speaks of the mother eagle many times, and God, in the above Scriptures, compared himself to a mother eagle. He says, "As she taketh them and beareth them on her wings, so I, the Lord, did lead thee," and "As the eagle stirreth up her nest, fluttereth over her young, spreadeth abroad her wings over them, taketh them and beareth them, so I bear you on eagles' wings."

The time comes for her little eagles to learn to fly, to get out of their nest and to get into God's great big blue sky where they belong. When they are not willing to do it, the Bible tells us how she gets them off the briar and gets them on the wing.

The Bible says that she stirreth up her nest. The eagle stirs her nest by using her claws and taking out all the downy feathers, the skins of animals, the rags, and the soft down. Then she lets the little eagles down on the sharp briars. There they become uneasy and scared. They have been raised in the comfort and ease of that nest. And now, all of a sudden, the mother takes the soft cover, rips it out, and lets them down in the bottom of the nest, right on the sharp briars. They twist and squirm. They become uncomfortable. Their little world has been turned upside down and they become afraid and uneasy. When this happens, the mother eagle lifts herself up over the nest a few feet and flutters or shakes out her wings. The naturalists say that the shaking and fluttering of those wings is a language that the little eagles understand. It is her way of comforting them and saying, "Everything is all right. Mother is here. Don't get alarmed. Don't get scared. I am here." And she quiets and calms them by the shaking of her wings. But this does not suffice. They are still uncomfortable, still uneasy. The nest is suddenly too little, too cramped, too uncomfortable, and they don't know what to think.

The Bible says that then she stretches abroad her wings. The wingspread of an eagle is very broad. My brother once killed an eagle and we took its wings and stretched them and measured them. They measured exactly 8 feet. I am told that some eagles in the countries of Asia have a wingspread of 14 feet. When you see an eagle with her wings folded together you would never guess how big she really is.

But now, when the little eagles become uncomfortable, scared, and uneasy, and the fluttering of the wings is not sufficient to quiet them, she rises above the nest and stretches abroad those wings. She hovers above them with those great, powerful pinions stretched out and gives them a glimpse of how big she is, how strong and capable she is, how she can pick them up, how she can take care of them. They never knew their mother was that big. They had felt the soft down of her feathers; they had seen her flutter and stretch her wings; but they had never seen her stretch them abroad like this. They had no idea how big their mother really was.

Then she lights on the side of the nest and lays down one of those wide, strong wings. She talks to them and says, "Get off the briar and get on the wing." If they won't leave the nest to get on the wing, she beats them with her wings. When they still won't leave the nest of briars and get on her wing, she won't give them any food. Pretty soon they think the world is ended. They have lost the covering, the soft down; they have lost their food; their mother has turned against them. A few minutes later she lays her big wing back down on the side of the nest and demands: "Get off the briar and get on the wing!" After a while one little eagle braves it and reaches out with its talons and catches hold of the wing. Another follows it, and another. Then suddenly she lurches forward, lifts herself, soars straight up, and begins to fly. Those little eagles hang on for dear life.

There she goes—up and up, mile after mile—soaring, flying, drifting, winging her way across the sky. The little eagles forget all about everything else from the sheer ecstasy of that flight. Up over the hills and into the deep blue of the sky, up and around and down they fly.

Then she brings them back and she puts her wing down. They jump off and get back into the nest only to find that the soft down is gone and they are right back on the briar. She puts her wing back down, and immediately they climb off the briar, get on her wing, and up she goes again. She comes back and dumps them off. They get back on, and up she goes. She keeps on until she takes away that fear.

Then one day, with them on her wings, she is soaring high above the earth. All of a sudden she lurches and knocks them off into the air. Those little eagles begin to scream and plummet toward the earth like a bullet, beating their wings and screaming at the tops of their voices. Before they hit the ground, the big mother eagle speeds downward with superb accuracy. Spreading out her wings under them, she catches them and up she goes again, high into the sky. She shakes them off, and then catches them up again until they stretch out their wings and find they can fly. There they go, side by side, flying, soaring, and gliding.

Then they go back to the nest. They scramble down on the briars, but they fly right back up. They fly up and they fly back. They look at the nest, then turn and go back up into the sky.

Then the day comes when they are done with that little nest of briars. Up and up they go to take their place in the sky. The mother eagle has one thing more for them. She takes them on some high mountain peak or some lofty, rocky crag. There she waits for bad weather because she wishes to teach them how to rise above the storm.

They say the eagle is the only bird that has a telescopic and microscopic eye. When the sun is shining in its greatest brilliance, the eagle can look straight into it and not blink an eye. They also have uncanny hearing. When a storm approaches, the eagle knows it long before the human being knows it. She scans the horizon, watching for telltale signs. When the wind begins to blow, the thunder begins to crash, the lightning flashes, she gets ready. As the winds increase their power and velocity, she spreads her wings in a certain way, bares her breast, and stands waiting. The winds that bring in the storm strike the set of her wings and lift her straight up above the storm, where she stays until the storm is over. Then she comes back down to her mountain home. Now that is the last thing she does for her youngsters who are learning to fly. She gets them off the briar and on the wing. She teaches them how to set their wings and bare their breasts so the wind will lift them above the storm.

God says this is the way he deals with people. He stirs our nest. He stirred the nest of the children of Israel while they were in bondage in Egypt. There they were in their nest in the land of Goshen. The most fertile soil of Egypt was theirs. They were prospering and getting along well. They were in favor of the king and he was in favor of them. They had become a mighty and powerful nation in the land of Egypt. But the time came when they were to stretch their wings and go back to the Land of Promise.

Jacob had brought his sons and his family down with him about 400 years prior to this at the invitation of Joseph, and the nation had been spared. Now the time has come for the great nation of Israel to be established. They shall be the instruments of God's mighty power among mankind. Through them the Saviour will be born. Through them a Messiah shall come forth from the tribe of Judah.

Here they are in Egypt. They are fast adopting the ways of Egypt. Soon they will lose their national identity. God speaks and stretches out his arms, and calls them to go up out of Egypt and return to the Land of Promise. But they turn a deaf ear to him. They like the soft comforts of Egypt. They are not willing to leave.

Then God stirred their nest. He took away the soft down and the lining. The Pharaoh who was favorable to them died. Another Pharaoh arose who didn't know them. The armies turned against them. The taskmasters turned against them. Pretty soon their lives were bitter with terrible persecution and sacrifice. As a result, they cried to God for deliverance. From one end of Goshen to the other they cried unto God night and day. They were cramped and uneasy, scared and miserable, for it seemed even God had forsaken them.

Here is what God was doing. He had called them, but they wouldn't go. They wouldn't go so there was only one thing left to do—stir their nest. The time comes for you and me to obey God, to launch out, to do what he has called us to do. If we refuse to do it, there is only one thing left for God to do, and that is to stir our nest, to take away the soft lining, to remove the cover and let us down on the briars. Then we can tell the difference between the briar and the wing and can see what God wants us to do.

Then the children of Israel were heard. God sent Moses. That was God's way of fluttering his wings. That was his way of saying, "I understand. I know what's going on. Don't be scared. Don't be uneasy." Then he stretched abroad his wings. He put a rod in Moses' hand and gave him the power to bring down seven plagues. Moses stretched out that rod and performed many signs and wonders, and stirred all the nation of Egypt. This was God stretching out his wings. This was God letting Israel know how big he is. They didn't know how big God is, how capable he is of taking care of and delivering his people.

They had been watched over by their friends in the government of Egypt, and now they are going to get a glimpse of the power of God. They had seen Pharaoh's power and found safety and security in it. Now all this is suddenly taken away from them and a new power is rising on the horizon—their God! His power is so vast that he scooped out the beds of the oceans, flung the stars from his finger tips, and hung the earth on nothing. He will roll back the waters of the Red Sea so they can cross dry-shod. God will rain down quail on toast and manna each day, six days a week. God will roll old Jordan back and bring the people across dry-shod.

God stretched out his hand and touched Moses at the burning bush. Moses walked through Egypt, defying Pharaoh, stretching out his rod and bringing down plagues. The angel was destroying the first-born of Egypt and sparing the first-born of God's people. It was a time when God was showing forth his mighty power.

The great campaigns of deliverance now abroad in the earth is God stretching out his wings. It is God showing us how big he is. The time has come for the church to launch out, for the people of God to get into a larger place, to turn their faith loose, and to receive power to perform signs, wonders, and mighty miracles. Every preacher who won't launch out, every church that will not wake up, every child of God who won't obey God is going to have his nest stirred. God will stretch out his wings and show the people how great and mighty he is. He will show us the far sweep of his eternal purpose, the magnitude and enormity of his power. He will roll back the enemies, stop the mouths of lions, help us escape the violence of the sword and the flame of the fire. God in all his wrath will come forth and reveal himself to his people. When you see a miracle of healing, when you feel the presence of God going through your mortal flesh, that's God stretching out his arms in these last days, releasing his power and showing forth his name among men.

God stirred their nest. How glad and happy they were to leave. He led them on out, and the time came when they didn't want to go back. They waved good-bye to the Egyptians' onion and garlic. They walked across old Jordan dry-shod. They had learned to fly. They had got off the briar and got on the wing.

A few years ago, God stirred my nest in Enid, Oklahoma. I was pastoring a good church, but God's time came for me to launch out and bring healing to multitudes of people. The time came for my ministry to burst open and bloom like a flower. The time came when God would send me from one end of America to the other in great campaigns attracting thousands and thousands of people to the Lord. The time came when he was to send me to the ends of the earth. I was to take this gospel of deliverance to millions of people who don't know Jesus Christ as a reality. He stirred my nest. He took away the soft down and cover and let me down on the briars. He made me so miserable, and the people so miserable about me, that when I got up and obeyed God, there was a sigh of relief all around.

God can make you so miserable, make other people so miserable about you, that when you do obey him everyone around you will be glad. In one week's time after I launched out, I was preaching to six and eight times the number of people I had been preaching to. In twelve months I was preaching to many more than that. In three years I was preaching to three, four, and five thousand people a night. Now, in our tent we are preaching to fifteen and eighteen thousand people a night. In the beginning of my ministry, I didn't have the great miracles I am having now. Every now and then there would be a flash of God's power. There would be a revelation of his purpose. There would be a tremendous miracle performed. Although it didn't happen to every person, occasionally a miracle would occur. God was stretching out his wings showing me what could be done if I would believe, if I could open my mind, if I could grasp the significance of the ministry of deliverance, if I would launch out and obey God. By the very acts of his power, he was giving me a preview of what he would do for me and through me a little later on.

God is stirring my nest in America. My first burden has been for my country. I suppose I will have a burden for America as long as I live in this world. He is leading me to go to the ends of the earth, because I have heard the Macedonian call and the man in the vision has said, "Come over and help us." God has stirred my nest. He has made me uncomfortable and miserable. I have had a drive in my soul which I cannot explain to anybody. It burns me like a fire; it blows me like a wind; it pounds me like a hammer; night and day it roars in my mind. I cannot get away from it. How powerful it is inside my being! God is saying, "Rise up, Son, get off the briar and get on the wing. You are called to a world ministry. Go into all the world and preach the gospel to every creature, not to just a few in America, but to every creature for the gospel of the kingdom must be preached to all nations as a witness, and then shall the end come." He is telling me that the end is coming. Man's days are numbered. Time is short. The night is approaching and the midnight hour is upon us.

God is stirring the church. The church has built a nest. She is in the nest. The time has come for the church to get big, because the devil's kingdom is big. Sin is big; sickness is big; fear is big; and the work of demons is big. The church is little—too little. So many of us in the church are content with our little handful of people. I know—I have been right there. Some of us are not content, however. We say that if it is right to win one soul, it is right to win two souls. We say that it is greater to win a hundred souls than ten souls or that it is greater to win a million souls than a thousand souls.

The time has come for us to enlarge our borders, lengthen our cords, and strengthen our stakes. The time has come for the church to rise up and be the head—not the tail. The time has come for the church not to be narrow and denominational, selfish and prejudiced toward each other and toward men, but to be big, to open its soul and take the world into its arms. There is uneasiness in the church. Preachers cannot explain to you the feelings which are going through their hearts and the rumblings within their churches. They are uneasy because God is removing the soft cover and lining. Things aren't going right. They can't solve their problems. There is always something rising up that nobody can solve. Yes, the world is on the briar. God is laying down his wings saying, "Get off the briar and get on the wing." The time has come for his church to rise up and get on that wing where God wants it.

The church is to give Jesus to humanity, not some doctrine but a Man—Jesus of Nazareth. The church is not just to preach precepts; the church is to give a Man to mankind —the Son of God—a Man alive and with power, with inspiration and with deliverance. Too long we have majored on precepts. We have preached our little doctrine, and we have indoctrinated our little handful. But we have driven the world away because the world doesn't like a small tight place. The world doesn't understand how Christian people can be so narrow in their outlook on life. Therefore, God is stirring the church because he wants the church to be big-souled, big-minded, big in outlook, big in faith, and big in power. God is also stirring individuals. When he can't get you and me as individuals to obey him, there is one thing left for him to do, and that is to stir our nest. He can make us so miserable; everything goes wrong; nothing goes right. You feel that you have lost your last friend, maybe that even God has forsaken you. Then all of a sudden, you see God near you. You see his power. God stretches out his wings to show you how big he is. He hasn't forsaken you. He has just taken away the cover, the soft down. He wants you to get off the briar and to get on the wing.

A person who is on the wing doesn't feel the briars. A person who is obeying God isn't little. A person who isn't close to God is always telling you what somebody has done to them. A preacher who isn't close to God is always telling you how his church or his deacon board is against him. But a preacher who is on the wing doesn't stay on the briar. He is up there where there are no briars. He is getting the job done. When you are on the wing there is a different atmosphere. The world is big, the vision is big, and the world's cry reaches your ears. You are too big to come down to something little. Your mind is too big to entertain gossip. Your soul is too big to fuss and quarrel with anybody.

Get off the briar and get on the wing. There is such a different atmosphere up there. It is a different place. You have ecstasy; you are happy; you are thrilled. Did you ever see a Christian who is happy and filled with sunshine and joy? He is on the wing. He is up there in that world of sunshine. He got off the briar. He has waved good-bye to a little narrow concept and is there where Jesus is, where the kingdom of God is. He is sitting with Christ in heavenly places. How cramped some of us are, how miserable. Get off the briar, friend, and get on the wing.

There is one more thing God is doing. He is teaching us to set our wings for the coming storm. The storm *fear* is coming. There is no doubt about that. The H-bomb and communism are the twin monsters of our society. They are creating fear and insecurity in man's heart. They are a preview of the violence of the kingdom of Antichrist that is fast approaching. Communism in its godless philosophy is only a preview of Antichrist's kingdom and the mark of the beast. The H-bomb is only a foretaste of the terrible weapons of destruction that shall come to this world in the battle of Armageddon. The storm is coming. But, when you get off the briar and get on the wing, God teaches you how to set your wings to face the storm and get ready for the coming of Jesus of Nazareth. You have anointing; you have power; you have guidance.

God is trying to teach us something. Get your eyes open and look. Get your ears open and listen. Open your Bibles and read. Prophecy is going to be fulfilled. Every Scripture will come to pass. There is to be an end of time, when the angel of God shall put one foot on the land and one on the sea and declare that time shall be no more. We are in the drama of the end-time. We must learn what to do. What does the mother eagle do? She lives in a high place. She listens, she looks, and she discerns the storm before it strikes. She sets her wings; she bares her breast; and she gets herself ready. The winds that bring in the thunder, lightning, and devastation and destruction strike her breast and wings and up she goes, straight up like a bullet, above the storm.

That's what God is teaching you and me. He is saying, "Get out of that little nest. Get up on a high place. Get victory in your soul. Get rid of your bondage. Throw off your bad habits, your evil desires, and your bad thoughts. Get your mind cleaned up and your soul on fire for God. Get your body healed and get an outreach for every race of mankind." God is saying, "Throw out your chest. Put your shoulders back. Get yourself set. Get ready."

Someone is coming before Antichrist. That One is Jesus Christ. Before the tribulation there is the rapture of the saints. If you don't know how to fly now, you will never fly in the rapture. Learn how to fly. Learn how to obey God. Learn how to soar in ecstasy in the spirit realm. Learn now, because the time is coming when he shall split the eastern skies. He shall reveal himself and the saints shall see him. He will say, "Come, my people," and from all over this world they will slip out of beds and out of graveyards. They will rise to meet Jesus in the air. Friends, you had better know how to fly now. You had better get in tune with the Infinite. You had better have something in your spirit that the world can't give and the world can't take away.

Every follower of Jesus must get on fire for God. He has to be so anointed and his soul so on fire that he can't stand still. He has to be enthusiastic. He must be winning souls. He must be healing the sick. Remember, you have to have something real in your soul. Sinner, you had better get saved and live right. You have to be filled with the Spirit and wholly sanctified and set apart for the service of God. *Get off the briar and get on the wing!*

9 Christianity Is a Healing Religion

When the even was come, they brought unto him many that were possessed with devils: and he cast out the spirits with his word, and healed all that were sick: that it might be fulfilled which was spoken by Esaias the prophet, saying, Himself took our infirmities, and bare our sicknesses (MATTHEW 8:16,17).

The Christian religion is a healing religion. It is different from all other religions. The distinguishing thing that makes it different is the person who founded it, Jesus Christ of Nazareth. He made it unlike all other religions. It is a healing religion.

The Christian religion brings healing to the soul, mind, and body. It heals the human being. It puts a new value upon his whole being. It lifts him from the power of sin, from the force of sickness and disease, from mental stress and demon power. It delivers him from fear and it makes him an integrated personality, whole through and through.

It was founded by Jesus Christ—Son of God, Son of man —who came into this world, born of a virgin. He was born of a virgin to give him a human body, but he had no human father. He was conceived of the Holy Ghost and locked in the womb of a pure, unmarried girl who gave him his flesh. But his Spirit is eternal so that he is Son of God and Son of man—born with a human body with all the capacities for human things; but born without sin, born without disease, born without mental illness, born without fear—a perfectly integrated, undivided human being—the world's perfect Man.

His first public act was to turn water into wine, and he has been changing things and people ever since. His second public act was the healing of the nobleman's son, and he has been healing people ever since. From that moment, during his earthly ministry of three and a half years, he spent two thirds of his earthly ministry healing the sick people. He touched them with his hands; he let them touch him. They were healed, the Bible says, of every disease. They were healed through and through—body, mind, and soul. Not only did Jesus heal the people, but he gave this healing power to his followers and said unto them, "As you go, preach the gospel and heal the sick."

When Christ was upon the earth, he did two things in his ministry. First, he preached the gospel, and second, he healed the people. Then he transmitted this power to his followers. He told them that they would heal the sick and cast out devils. He said, "And these signs shall follow them that believe . . . they shall lay hands on the sick, and they shall recover" (Mark 16:17,18). In fact, Jesus gave a new dimension in two ways to mankind: first, to man's whole body; and second, to the hand of man.

Jesus showed that man is not a physical being alone; man is not a mental being alone; man is not a spiritual being alone—man is all three. Man is soul, mind, and body, each having its particular importance. God gave the soul, and God made the body. He connected the two with the human mind so that all three are very important not only to the person, but also to the Almighty God himself.

Religion is not exclusively for the soul. It is for the soul, but it is also for the mind and the body. Jesus put a new value upon the whole being of man. Nothing about man is unimportant. Everything about man is of value. He forgave his sins; he delivered him from his fears; he healed him from his sicknesses. And the Bible says they were made every whit whole. *Every whit whole!* Jesus gave a new dimension to the whole being of man.

Second, he gave a new dimension to the hand of man. He said, "These signs shall follow them that believe; In my name . . . they shall lay hands on the sick, and they shall recover" (Mark 16:17,18). Not only is man a whole being; not only is God concerned about healing the whole being of man, but God is concerned that each man, each woman, shall be a healer—that each shall practice the Christian religion. The founder of the Christian religion is a healer; therefore, the followers of that man shall be healers. They shall be deliverers; they shall be saviors; they shall be salt to the earth and light to the world. They shall lay hands upon the sick, *and they shall recover!* Somehow the power of God was transmitted through the hands of the followers of Christ. They went out and laid hands on the sick and these sick people were healed. Today we lay hands upon the sick and they are healed. There is a new dimension for the hand of man.

It is significant to me that the last act of Christ before his crucifixion was the healing of the ear of Malchus with a touch of his hand. Jesus showed man that his hand was not to be balled into a fist to strike another, but it is to be stretched out to heal and to bless.

The hand of man is a healing instrument—your doctor's hands, your mother's hands, the hand of a friend, the hand of a beloved person, the hand of your little child—especially if the spirit of the person whose hand is outreached is filled with love. If the person is the right kind of person inside, he communicates through his hands. The very emotion of the inner man is expressed through the hands. Don't you remember when your mother put her hands on you? Isn't it a marvelous feeling when you approach a friend who is in trouble, or a loved one who is in need of a good word, and shake their hand? You get hold of that person's hand with your hand, and you express yourself. Don't you communicate something to that person? Isn't there a healing influence in your hand?

The followers of Christ have healing to give to their fellow man. This is quite a new idea. We have been led to believe that there is nothing that can be received physically, that we are not to expect a miracle, that healing is not to be practiced. But that is not the Bible, nor the Christian religion. We are coming back to the original concept of Christ. We are bringing back early Christianity and giving it to the world.

How does the Christian religion bring healing? First, healing is through a Person, Jesus of Nazareth. You are healed, not just through a philosophy, or a theology, or an attitude; you are healed through a Person—a Man, a living Man, who was crucified but rose from the dead, who is alive right now at his Father's right hand. You were healed through a Man. We pray in the name of Jesus of Nazareth, Son of God and Son of man. The Christian religion heals not in itself but through faith in Jesus the founder.

What do we understand about Jesus? We read in our text that "Himself took our infirmities, and bare our sicknesses." So the fulfillment of prophecy is that Christ took our infirmities, and bare our sicknesses. If Christ took my infirmities and bore them in his own body on the cross of Calvary, why must I carry them now? If he took my sins, why do I carry my sins? If he can forgive my sin, why then can he not heal my sickness? He does forgive my sin; he does heal my sickness—because he took my infirmities and he bore my sickness. Christ himself was never in sin; he never was sick; he never had a demon; he never was filled with fear. Therefore, he does not want me to have sin or a demon. He does not want me to be filled with fear. He does not want me to carry sickness in my body. He wants me to be like him. God wants me to be like Jesus in body, mind, and soul, so that I, instead of being sick, can do what he told me to do—lay my hands on the sick that they may recover.

The Christian religion is a dynamic thing. It has striking power; it is full of healing virtue. The Christian religion is the outstretched hands of the followers of Christ. It is the outstretched hand of the founder, Jesus Christ. The Christian religion is the power of God brought to bear upon the torments of the human being.

We understand also that Christ is full of healing power. In the eighth chapter of Luke and the fifth chapter of Mark we have the story of the woman with the issue of blood. She said, "If I may touch but the hem of Christ's garment, I shall be whole." And when she touched his clothes with her hand, she turned her faith loose and she believed. He felt healing power go out of him. That is the way he knew that she was healed.

We know that we are healed through a Person. Christ is full of healing power. To touch him is to be healed; for him to touch you is to be healed. The only way you won't be healed is to fail to understand *that he is a healer.* You can embrace the Christian religion without being healed. If you don't know healing exists, then certainly you are not going to believe for it. You can't believe for something that you don't know you can have. But when you understand that the Christian religion is a healing religion, then you are going to ask for healing, believe for it, and receive it. It is for you!

God healed me of tuberculosis and a stuttering tongue, and said, "Son, be like Jesus and heal the people as he healed them." That is what I'm trying to do. I know I'm not as good as Jesus. I know I'm not perfect like Jesus, but I'm trying to be like him. I'm trying to heal just as he did, through the power of God. It is God who heals, not I. God heals, I don't; but I am an instrument that God is using, and I am a point of contact for millions of people in these last days. I am raised up to show people that the Christian religion is a healing religion because the founder is the healer —the Great Physician of the human family.

We understand also that we are healed through a Person, because he has authority over all sickness and disease. In Matthew 28:18 he said, "All power is given unto me in heaven and in earth." Not 50 per cent of the power; not 99 per cent of the power, but *all* power in Heaven and in earth! He has all power over all sickness and disease which means that we are healed through a Person.

Second, we are healed through the Word of God. The Bible says, "He sent his *word,* and healed them" (Psalm 107:20). The Word of God is a book of life. We understand by faith that when he spoke the creative word, the world came into being. The word of God has creative power. The word of God has power to change the world. It has life in it. God spoke it; men heard it, and wrote it down in a book which we have today as the Holy Bible.

Therefore, he heals through his word. When I speak by the anointing of the Spirit of God, my words have power. They have life. They move people and they change people. They bring people to a decision and move them to action. And how much more, if my word has power, does God's Word have power.

We are healed by the Holy Bible as we read it. It reveals the promises of God to each of us. It solves the riddles of life for all of us. The Holy Bible gives answers to our problems, shows us the way, the truth, and the life.

Third, we are healed through the followers of Jesus. Jesus said to his followers, "Greater things than these shall ye do, because I go to my Father." It is a very outstanding statement. We read of what Christ did, and how he did it, and then he has the courage to say, "Ye shall do greater things." It means that the followers of Christ are given power to do greater things, and we are doing greater things. That may sound sacrilegious to you, but I feel very humble when I say it. We are simply obeying the Lord and doing what he told us to do.

In this modern age of skepticism and unbelief, we are having great revivals. We are seeing thousands of people saved, thousands healed, and we are seeing it in spite of the devil's opposition. We are seeing it in spite of the fact that many don't believe the Christian religion is a healing religion. Jesus gave his followers power. He said, "I give unto you power to heal all manner of sickness and disease, to cast out devils, and to do these wonderful things." They got the power; they used the power; they laid their hands upon the sick, and the people were healed of diseases and demons. They returned with great joy saying, "Lord, even the devils are subject unto us through thy name."

Why should a Christian not heal today? Has Christ changed? Has the Bible changed? Has the Christian religion changed? No! The very moment that you and I become like Christ, we have the power to heal.

Now you say, "Brother Roberts, do you have perfect power?"

No, I don't. I don't know that I'll ever get perfect power in this world, because I am a man. I'm not God.

You say, "Are all the people you pray for healed?"

Apparently they are not. Some people we pray for receive no healing, or at least their healing isn't evident to us.

You say, "Are any healed?"

By the multiplied thousands!

You ask me for my proof. I don't try to prove it. I just say, "There's the person. Let him tell you."

You say, "That is no proof to me."

Maybe it isn't to you, but it is to me—and to the person. You see the point? I don't argue religion with anybody. I don't force my religion on anybody. I do what I believe is right. If a person is healed, that evidence satisfies me and it satisfies them.

You ask me what diseases are healed.

All manner of diseases and all conditions are healed.

You ask me what types of sin are healed.

All kinds of sin are healed.

What kind of demons are cast out of people?

All kinds of demons are cast out.

God does not limit himself to hands. He heals by association, by communication.

What do we mean by *association?* Well, the robe that Jesus wore had no healing power, but a woman said, "If I can touch it, I'll be healed." And she was! She associated the robe with his power. Paul took the handkerchief from his pocket and sent it to be laid upon the sick. People took the handkerchief and associated it with the Apostle Paul. He said, "I can't be there in person. If I could, I'd lay my hand upon you, but here is the next best thing. Take this handkerchief, which comes from my body, put it on you, and let it be as though Paul stood there." By association they turned their faith loose and were healed. We are healed through association. The shadow of Peter was a healing power through association. He walked down the street and his shadow fell upon sick people. They associated the shadow with him, turned their faith loose, and they were healed.

If you believe strong enough in the prayers of any Christian, and they can't get to you or you can't get to them, if you could even touch their clothes, through that association you could turn your faith loose and be healed. It is as simple as can be.

The Christian religion brings you healing by a *person*, by the *word of that person*, and by *association*. Why, God uses my voice on the radio; he uses my presence on a TV film; he uses little cloths which we pray over and send out; he uses my writings, my magazines, my books; he uses my hand. Why, I just let the Lord use anything I have. If he will use it, I gladly give it to him. "Freely ye have received, freely give" (Matthew 10:8). The main thing is to believe and let God have his way.

What is the best way to get healed? How may the Christian religion actually bring healing to you right now? First, you must accept Jesus Christ as your Saviour—the Lord and God of your life. If you want the Christian religion, you must accept the founder of the Christian religion, who is Jesus Christ. Second, you must be born again, born by the Spirit of God, born from above. You must have a new life. By your sins, you are dead. You may have life in your body, but there is death in your soul.

You must be born a second time. You were born the first time of your mother by physical birth. You must now be born a second time by spiritual birth. You must come to God and repent of your sins and believe on Jesus. When you believe on Jesus you will be born a second time. You will know when you come into the new birth. You will have life flowing through your being by the miraculous power of God. The new birth is a dynamic experience. It is something you can feel. Can a newborn baby feel life? Can a newborn baby cry? Can a newborn baby use its hands? Does a newborn baby have life flowing through it? Just so, when a person is born the second time by the Spirit of God, he receives life. He knows it! He feels it!

You say, "Brother Roberts, I have never felt that." Then you are not saved. If you have never felt the Spirit of God, please tell me how you knew when you came to life. How did you know when you got it? How would you know if you lost it? My friend, when you believe, something happens.

You may belong to a church. But I'm saying to you that you can be born again, and that they are two different ideas altogether. You are saved by believing on a Man, Jesus Christ. You are not saved by joining a church. You join a church so you can have other Christian people to fellowship with, but you are saved by faith in Christ. You must be born again by his Spirit.

What has that got to do with the healing of your body? It deals with the question of sin, which is the root of all your trouble. You must settle the sin question, and quit living wrong. You can't quit living wrong until you repent of sin and God saves you from it. The new birth is a deliverance from sin.

You know, you can belong to a church and still be on the devil's side. You must have Jesus in your heart; you must know that the Lord lives in your soul. You need a salvation that will deliver you from the crown of your head to the soles of your feet; you need God to take the sin out of you, the devil out of you, and the fear out of you, to change your life and to come into your heart.

You need something that will put a shine on your face, a twinkle in your eye, a shout in your soul, a lift to your shoulder, a spring in your step. You need something to make the angels sing in your soul, to make Heaven your home, God your Father, the Holy Ghost your Comforter, Jesus your Saviour, the angels your guides, and the saints your brothers and sisters. You need something that will give you a title to a mansion in the sky. You need power to live for God seven days a week. You need the glory of God in your heart. "*Ye must be born again*" (John 3:7).

You can be healed; first, by accepting the Person of Jesus Christ; second, by being born again; and third, by turning your faith loose.

Picture your faith as a giant that you have chained. He is powerful, but you have him chained. Unchain him, turn him loose; let him work for you. You may accept Jesus as your Saviour, and be born again, and still not be healed from sickness. Because the third thing has to be done, you must turn your faith loose.

How are you healed? "The prayer of faith shall save the sick" (James 5:15). Some of the people who come to my meetings don't get healed, because they think I am the healer. They think if they can come in my line, I will heal them. I don't heal; I can't heal; only God can heal. I am an instrument that God uses. My hands are used of God, but they are used by faith—by faith alone. It is faith that heals the sick.

We release our faith by a point of contact; if I step on the starter of my car, I expect the motor to start. You turn your faucet and water comes out. That is the point of contact. You flip a light switch, light comes on. That is the point of contact. You must have a point of contact to turn your faith loose. The point of contact sets the time for you to believe. Some people don't get healed because they don't set the time to be healed. The point of contact sets the time. My right hand is a point of contact. My voice is a point of contact. The back of a chair in our big tent can be a point of contact. A handkerchief on your body can be a point of contact. The Bible can be a point of contact. The laying of your hand on the radio during my broadcast can be a point of contact. Anything is a point of contact if it helps you turn your faith loose.

Some people say, "Brother Roberts, pray a long time for me. I'm really sick." I don't pray hours for one person. There are millions of people whom I want to reach. I don't want to spend all my time with one person. I'm trying to reach the masses for Christ. I'm not satisfied to reach a handful. I want to reach the world. I can't save you. I can't heal you. Only God can save and heal. I am to help you release your faith. I am an instrument that God is using. Let me pray for you. Let me preach to you. Let's believe. God will set you free!

Will You Make the March of Faith . . . Now?

10

And there were four leprous men at the entering in of the gate: and they said one to another, Why sit we here until we die? (2 KINGS 7:3).

This is a message to those people who are hemmed in by some awful power like sickness, fear, frustration, inner conflict, defeat, failure, hunger, or poverty. It is a message of hope to everyone who needs deliverance by the power of faith in God.

The city of Samaria was besieged by the Syrian army which had cut off the food supply. Food was so scarce that some of the people were eating the flesh of their own children. A cry was raised for the prophet Elisha to bring deliverance to the city. When approached by the elders the prophet prophesied that deliverance would come tomorrow and that the deliverance would be so great and food so plentiful that a bushel of flour, which was then unobtainable, would sell for only a few pennies. Elisha prophesied that the Syrians would be utterly defeated and driven away and that all of their food supply would be given to the people of Samaria.

For days the city had been shut up while famine stalked the land and people died by the thousands. Elisha prophesied such a great deliverance within twenty-four hours. One of the servants of the king mocked the prophet and said, "Behold, if the Lord would make windows in heaven, might this thing be?"

Elisha turned upon this doubter and said, "Behold, thou shalt see it with thine eyes, but shalt not eat thereof."

There wasn't a man, or woman, or child in the city of Samaria who believed the prophecy of Elisha. But Elisha lived close to God and knew that God would deliver his people. After uttering his prophecy, he waited for God to go to work.

Sitting at the gate of the city were four leprous men who were destined to be God's instruments to fulfill Elisha's promise of deliverance. They didn't know they were the ones. They knew only that they were sick, starving, dying men surrounded by famine and the Syrian army. They were hopeless.

The four men had not heard the prophecy of Elisha. They did not know that deliverance was coming by the hand of the Lord. They did not know that tomorrow food would be plentiful. They knew only that they were starving to death.

These four men have become unique in history because in their extremity they rose up and marched against the Syrian army. As they sat at the entrance of the gate they asked themselves a question, a question that comes ringing down through centuries: "Why sit we here until we die?"

They could have asked themselves needless, unanswerable questions. They could have asked, "Why has this happened to us? What have we done to deserve it?" Instead they asked, "Why sit we here until we die?"

How many times do people defeat themselves by torturing their minds with needless, unanswerable questions? When trouble or sickness, or some other calamity comes upon us, we usually say, "Why did this happen to me? What have I done to deserve it?" There is only one question the human being should ask himself about his troubles, "Why sit I here until I die?"

Who can explain the troubles, the afflictions, the torments that come to us? Who has the answer to the why of man's sufferings? I am frank to say that I do not have the answer to all the whys of life. There is one thing I do know, however. We don't have to sit until we die. We can rise up and do something about our situation.

Friends, all of us have faith. We are taught that in Romans 12:3 where Paul said, "God hath dealt to every man the measure of faith." We have the faith for the problems and situations in life. Why do we sit until we die? Why do we not rise up and believe? Jesus said, "All things are possible to him that believeth."

One of the things we are prone to forget when we are in trouble is the presence of God that is everywhere in the universe. God is omnipresent. He is not only present everywhere at the same time but he is present everywhere to bless humanity. The Bible says, "He that cometh to God must believe that he is, and that he is a rewarder of them that diligently seek him" (Hebrews 11:6). You can make contact with the presence of God anywhere, at any time of day or night. The question we should ask ourselves is not, "Why has this happened to me, or what have I done to deserve it?" We should ask ourselves, "Why sit we here until we die?"

The four leprous men decided to get up and do something. The Bible described their action as follows: *And there were four leprous men at the entering in of the gate: and they said one to another, Why sit we here until we die? If we say, We will enter into the city, then the famine is in the city, and we shall die there: and if we sit still here, we die also. Now therefore come, and let us fall unto the host of the Syrians: if they save us alive, we shall live; and if they kill us, we shall but die* (2 Kings 7:3,4).

They reasoned that if they remained sitting at the gate they would die by famine; likewise, if they entered the city, because of the famine there. There was one hope, and that was to rise and march upon the Syrians. If the Syrians would receive them, they should live. If they killed them, they were going to die anyway.

That evening, while Samaria starved, four gaunt, sick, hungry, dying men rose up, and in the twilight started their march toward the Syrian army. *They began their march of faith.*

Few people have ever been delivered from sin, sickness, fear, or any other awful power who have not made the march of faith.

Look at these four men.

They were hungry, but they marched on.

They were sick, but they marched on.

They were dying, but they marched on.

They were tortured with pain, but they marched on.

They were stalked with danger and death, but they marched on.

They were alone in the night, but they marched on.

Every step was agony, but they marched on.

Occasionally they would stagger and stumble and would have to help each other. At times all four of them had to cling to each other to keep from falling, but they had decided that if they were going to die anyway they weren't going to sit and wait for it. They were going to make the march of faith and fall upon the Syrians. If they died, they would die as men of action and men with faith in their hearts.

A multitude of soldiers was camped around the city of Samaria, hundreds of thousands of men with their horses and chariots of war. They were in complete control of the city and were now making final plans to invade and destroy it. The night the four men made their march of faith the Syrians were asleep because they were not expecting an outside attack. But God, who never sleeps, saw the four faith-marchers coming. Each man was skin and bones, but in his heart was faith. That was all God needed and wanted. He went to work.

What can four hopeless men marching in the night hope to accomplish against a mighty army of the Syrians? It is not what four hopeless men can do, it is what God can do.

God made the faith march of these four men sound like a mighty army!

The Syrians were awakened in their tents by the sound of a mighty host. They heard what appeared to be a mighty army, but in reality the sound they heard was God working through the four faith-marchers.

The four men in their march of faith, so weak that they stumbled and fell every few steps, became the army of God. God made their stumbling steps sound like the precision marching of a million soldiers, like the hoofbeats of thousands of horses, like the earth-shaking roar of thousands of iron chariots. As the four men whispered encouragement to each other God made their whispers in the night sound like a great shout of victory, like a mighty noise of triumph.

Suddenly, the Syrians were awakened in their tents by the terrible sounds of this mighty army. Fear struck them. They arose up and fled in the night, leaving the whole camp empty.

The four men didn't know they sounded like a mighty host. They were making the march of faith because they believed it was their only hope. Their faith was the faith of desperation. Having come to the end of themselves, they knew their only hope was in their faith. No doubt many a shiver shook their frame and many a doubt assailed their faith. Terrors of the night cast their shadows before them. They didn't know exactly where the camp was, only that it was out there somewhere in the night. The dread mystery of the unknown gripped their hearts. None of these things stopped them because they were not willing to sit until they died.

What made the difference?

They didn't know where the Syrians were located, but God did.

They didn't know they would ever make it to the outer camp, but God did.

They didn't know they weren't going to die on the way, but God did.

They didn't know their stumbling in the night would sound like a mighty host of chariots and horses, or that their whispers in the dark would sound like the shout of triumph of a mighty host, but God did.

They didn't know that Elisha had prophesied victory for the next day, but God did.

They didn't know that they were supposed to wait until the next day before they had anything to eat, but God did.

They didn't know that it could be done, but God did.

They arose and said, "Come on, let's go."

It is said that it is a scientific impossibility for a bumblebee to fly. They say its body is too heavy for its wings, but the bumblebee doesn't know it. So it goes ahead and flies anyway and makes a little honey while it does it. The four men didn't know that they had to wait until the next day to get deliverance. So they obtained it the night before.

Friend, you don't have to wait until you have a better opportunity to be delivered. You don't have to wait until someone comes to your community praying for the sick to be healed. You don't have to wait until you are older, or until your circumstances change, or until you move to some other location, in order to better your life. You don't have to wait at all. Rise up and make the march of faith, and you can have deliverance right now.

You don't even have to wait until you finish reading this chapter. You can lay this book upon your body as a point of contact, raise your hands to Heaven, turn your faith loose, and God will bless you from the top of your head to the soles of your feet.

The four men marched into the camp of the Syrians and found it deserted. They couldn't understand what had happened. They had heard the rumbling of the chariots of war and the voices of the Syrians for many weeks. Now the camp was empty and silent. They rushed from tent to tent finding food, gold, silver, and plenty of everything else. Then they said to each other, "This day is the day of good tidings. Now therefore come, that we may go and tell the king's household."

The four men, who had stumbled and staggered in the night clinging to each other for faith and hope in their desire to fall upon the Syrians, now returned to the city in great triumph. They were able to run and to shout that victory was theirs. The city was awakened and the king notified. Then the people marched on the camp of the Syrians. By daylight the city was full of food. The people were singing and dancing in the streets and the prophecy of Elisha had come to pass.

There was only one solemn, sad note in the whole affair. The man who doubted the prophecy of Elisha was appointed to man the gates, and as he tried to restrain the people in their gladness he was trodden underfoot and killed. Because of his doubt, Elisha had said unto him, "Behold, thou shalt see it with thine eyes, but shalt not eat thereof." He died without a morsel of the food the four leprous men had found.

What was true back there is true today. God has promised deliverance to all of us. He has promised to save us, to heal us, to prosper us, to give us life, and to give it to us more abundantly. Some doubt, and although they will see it with their eyes, they will not partake of it. But those who believe it, and reach out to receive it, will be blessed beyond their fondest dreams and expectations.

Remember this, no one knows what our faith sounds like to the devil.

11 The Religious Revival of Today and What It Means

Very many people are writing to me and saying, "Brother Roberts, what does this great spiritual resurgence of faith throughout the world mean? What does it stand for? What is its true significance?" There is a Scripture in the Book of Acts which reads, *It shall come to pass in the last days, saith God, I will pour out of my Spirit upon all flesh* (Acts 2:17). Look at the last two words of this prophecy: "I will pour out of my Spirit upon *all flesh*."

From the standpoint of man, the religious revival today means one thing, and from the standpoint of God, it means entirely another thing.

First, I wish to discuss it from man's standpoint. It means man's distrust of man. Man doesn't trust himself. He never has. Cain didn't trust his brother Abel. When men built the tower of Babel they didn't trust either themselves or God. Since that time there has been a vast distrust in the hearts of men everywhere. Men have built the hydrogen bomb because they distrust each other. They are afraid of the intent of their fellow men. That is why we have wars. Wars are a symptom of man's distrust of man. Subconsciously man is recognizing his need of supernatural deliverance from other men, from the problems that he brings upon himself. So this great religious revival of our time, from man's standpoint, means that man distrusts man, and that he is subconsciously turning to a higher power to solve his problems.

Also, it means that man is recognizing his own inadequacy before the threats of nature such as floods, hurricanes, earthquakes. Never in my life have I witnessed or heard of such vast floods and terrible hurricanes and earthquakes throughout this earth. In the face of the threats of nature and the violence of the elements, man is unconsciously turning back to God and realizing that he cannot protect himself even from the forces of nature.

Man is realizing his own failure to bring himself peace of soul and peace of mind. In this world there is not much peace. Men cry *peace and safety*, but there is no peace in the hearts of men and women. Man is now realizing that he is unable to bring peace to his own mind and soul. Therefore, he is turning to the power of the Prince of Peace, Jesus Christ of Nazareth.

It means, also, that man is failing to heal himself. In spite of the great strides that medical science is making, mankind is sick. We've never known such sickness in the world as we see now. I've traveled in most of the continents of the earth. I have preached before great masses of humanity and I know that now, more than ever before, there is a great urge in man's heart to seek divine healing. Man is taking advantage of all that medical science has to offer. But with all that, he is turning to divine healing as he never has in his history.

Then it means something else. From man's standpoint the revival means that at last his faith is becoming aroused. He is finally coming to realize that he is basically a spiritual being.

Christ said, "Man shall not live by bread alone." This means that man basically is a spiritual being. He has a body, but he is not physical. He has a mind, but he's not mental. Man is a spiritual being, for God breathed into his nostrils the breath of life and he became a living soul. That living soul is in need of spiritual things. He has a tremendous spiritual capacity which God alone can fill and satisfy. In this world of material things where man is ever in a search for material things, such as bread, and wealth, houses and lands, stocks and bonds, there arises within him that terrific spiritual urge, which no amount of bread or no measure of material things can satisfy. Out of the depths of his being his spiritual nature is expressing itself. It is reaching up and reaching out to the living God, who alone can satisfy the basic urges of man's life.

So the religious revival today from man's standpoint means that man is turning away from himself to the great Creator, to the Author of life, to the Originator of the things that count the very most in life.

Now, I wish to discuss the religious revival today from the standpoint of Almighty God. First, it means that the time has come for man's regeneration. Man has been incapable of realizing this need before now. He has been so carried away with his own powers, so prone to magnify his own genius, that he has not been in a position to accept the fact that he needed God. He has his United Nations. He has his A-bomb and H-bomb. He has the power to sit down in a conference of nations and bring forth from himself the answer to many of his problems. In recognizing his own power and skill, he has failed to realize that he needed God.

Now he is seeing the end of his own efforts. He is seeing the failure of his own results. He is realizing just how inadequate he is to face the demands of his life. In fact, the works of nature such as floods and hurricanes and earthquakes, the threat of the H-bomb that hangs over his life all the time, the feeling of inadequacy within himself, all these things point to the time; and that time is now. You say, "Brother Roberts, hasn't God been ready all the time?" Yes; but in a sense man limits God and man determines when God deals with him. Water may be constant, but if you don't turn the hydrant on, water will not come out. Electricity is constant, but if you don't flip the light switch, electricity will not flow through to create light. The power of God is constant through the centuries. It is always available, but unless you come in contact with it, unless you get in harmony with it, unless you express your desire for it, unless you open your heart to receive it, the power of God, which is constant, will not come into you.

There are people who are seeking and finding God today. But because one person finds God in a remarkable way is no sign that the average person finds him like that or can find him like that.

The only time that any mass of people can find God is when the time is right—not necessarily from God's standpoint, but from man's standpoint. Man has to get in harmony with God. He has to have the desire for God. He has to want what God has to offer. But the tragedy is, man is not going to want what God has to offer until what he has provided for himself has failed. Therefore, in the failure of man, God's time has come. Never have we seen that time so right as this very second.

Also, from God's standpoint it means that God is bruising the serpent's head. In the very beginning of the human race, after the fall of man, God said to the woman that the devil would work against humanity, but that the seed of this woman would bruise the serpent's head. In my estimation the great spiritual revival today is a renewal of God's promise to us that he will defeat the devil, that he will bruise the serpent's head.

What does the religious revival mean for the future? First, it means a division of nations, of groups, of families, of individuals. Second, it means a beginning of the literal and complete witnessing to all nations and every creature, which will bring the end of time. Third, it means the mass miracle for millions is dawning. And fourth, it means the coming of Christ.

The spiritual revival, this tremendous resurgence of faith in the hearts of millions throughout the earth, can only mean that we are now seeing the literal and complete witnessing of Christ and for Christ to all nations and every creature. The Bible says, "This gospel of the kingdom shall be preached in all the world for a witness unto all nations; and then shall the end come" (Matt. 24:14). The end is near. We are now seeing a witnessing to all nations and every creature. It means the mass miracle for millions is about to happen and the coming of Christ is much nearer than we have realized.

What does this mean to us as individuals? It means that you and I must ever press toward God's kingdom. We must open our hearts to God. We must believe in him from a personal standpoint. We must walk and talk with the Lord, day after day. Right now, while my heart is stirred, while I feel God's anointing upon my being, I would like to reach forth my hand while you place your hand upon this book as a point of contact, and let me pray the prayer of faith with you and for you, that God will ever lead you and bring you close to him, that he will heal your body, that he will save your soul and that he'll especially come to you at this time. Will you believe with me? Accept him and his power for your personal need right now!